FARM FOLK

CITY FOLK

Stories, Tips and Recipes Celebrating Local Food
for Food Lovers of All Stripes

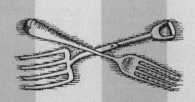

Herb Barbolet, Angela Murrills & Heather Pritchard
Photographs by Michael Marrapese

Douglas & McIntyre
Vancouver/Toronto

The authors would like to thank all the wonderful staff and volunteers at FarmFolk/CityFolk and everyone named in this book who gave so unstintingly of their time, knowledge and occasionally bed and board. Very special thanks to Bill Jones for his extraordinary help and enthusiasm; to Gurjit Sandhu of the Museum of Anthropology for opening the door to her culture; and to Michael Marrapese for much-appreciated assistance with recipe testing.

Douglas & McIntyre Ltd.
1615 Venables Street
Vancouver, British Columbia
V5L 2H1

Canadian Cataloguing in Publication Data

Barbolet, Herb.
  Farm folk, city folk

  ISBN 1-55054-651-1

  1. Food industry and trade—British Columbia. 2. Food. 3. Cookery, Canadian—British Columbia style. I. Murrills, Angela.
II. Pritchard, Heather. III. Title.
HD9014.C33B75 1998   641.3'009711   C98-910595-4

Editing by Barbara Pulling
Editorial consulting by Terri Wershler and Kelly Mitchell
Cover and text design by Gabi Proctor/DesignGeist
Cover photographs by Michael Marrapese
Photographs pages 49, 50 and 52 courtesy Nancy Turner
Printed and bound in Canada by Transcontinental Printing and Graphics, Inc.
Printed on acid-free paper ∞

The publisher gratefully acknowledges the support of the Canada Council for the Arts and of the British Columbia Ministry of Tourism, Small Business and Culture. The publisher also acknowledges the financial support of the Government of Canada through the Book Publishing Industry Development Program.

Grateful acknowledgement is made for permission to reprint recipes from the following books, all published by Douglas & McIntyre: *Bishop's: The Cookbook* by John Bishop. Copyright © 1996 by John Bishop. *HeartSmart Flavours of India* by Krishna Jamal. Copyright © 1998 by Heart and Stroke Foundation of Canada and Krishna Jamal. *Umberto's Kitchen: The Flavours of Tuscany* by Umberto Menghi. Copyright © 1995 by Umberto Menghi.

To the people who provide us with our food today, and to those working to ensure that food for future generations is safe, wholesome, nutritious and affordable

To my loving partner, Lynne—H.B.

To Peter, for his continual sustenance—A.M.

To my grandmother, Anna Neufeld, a wonderful gardener who created some of my earliest food memories—H.P.

Contents

Introduction

More than a decade ago, I moved from the hustle and bustle of the Kitsilano neighbourhood of Vancouver to an infinitely varied ten-acre farm near Aldergrove, in British Columbia's Fraser Valley. The farm is forty miles, one hour and a lifestyle away from the city. My move satisfied me in many ways, but attempting to maintain my urban income by commuting, consulting and teleconferencing proved difficult. So I did what most self-respecting community activists would do, faced with the need to earn a living: I got together with a few others, including my friend and colleague Heather Pritchard, and wrote an application for a grant to explore how small landholders could supplement their incomes.

Our year-long study introduced us to a hidden world of food producers, people creating wonderful treats for a small but discerning market. Pheasants, quail, pot-bellied pigs, hundred-year-old apple varieties, pea sprouts, nettle honey, and dozens of varieties of vegetables and medicinal and culinary herbs were tucked away in barns, garages, basements and back yards throughout the valley. Small processors, nursery owners, gardening book publishers and other entrepreneurs were busy creating both delectable morsels and fulfilling work for themselves. This was an underground economy worth knowing.

Today, that small number of producers has blossomed into quite a remarkable community. Since Expo 86 introduced us to the world, British Columbia's Lower Mainland has changed a great deal, but our province has fared better than most regions when it comes to the negative effects of globalization and corporate concentration. In many parts of the world these forces have created economies where everything is for sale and nothing is sacred. Perhaps, despite our temperate climate and spectacular natural beauty, our small population on an enormous land base makes us less attractive to transnational corporations seeking to exploit new markets. B.C. also has many activists who continue to fight fiercely for the preservation of our environment. While less than 5 per cent of the land in B.C. is capable of growing crops, even on a small commercial scale, our agricultural land has been protected from rapacious development for more than twenty-five years by an Agricultural Land Reserve.

By coincidence or not, after Expo there emerged a cadre of great British Columbia chefs, some of whom have gone on to win gold medals at the International Culinary Olympics. The thing these chefs have in common is their preference for fresh, local and in-season ingredients. Utilizing the resources B.C. has to offer, they have created a unique regional cuisine. Our lands and waters can, and do, produce virtually every foodstuff found anywhere in Canada (with the possible exception of the Arctic), and some food grown nowhere else in the country. In this book you'll even meet a grower producing bananas in his greenhouses, and back-yard gardeners in well-sheltered maritime areas are now growing bananas outdoors, along with dates and figs. Well over a hundred different commodities are cultivated and marketed in the Lower Mainland alone. In addition to ingenious agricultural and aquacultural products, there is the natural bounty of the place, from the unearthly gooseneck barnacle to the rare heritage crab apple. *Farm Folk, City Folk* brings you up close to some of the fascinating people who are working and—contrary to what your mother taught you—playing with food in British Columbia today. They talk about the joys and difficulties of their vocations, share tips on everything from composting to storing produce, and offer tantalizing recipes based on the fruits of their labours.

FarmFolk/CityFolk, the Vancouver-based organization from which this book takes its title, was created out of an awareness that local products, no matter how spectacular, can only be successful if a market is found for them. With McCulture quickly destroying the consumer's appreciation for quality, education and countermarketing are required to reintroduce people to the glories of their immediate surroundings. FarmFolk/CityFolk's goal is the creation of a just and sustainable food system, and the ideas we want to communicate are at once simple and profound. Our work on policy initiatives at the global level is the roux that binds together small-scale, tangible projects on a neighbourhood-by-neighbourhood basis and makes the whole mixture a delicate and delicious stew. Three concepts are central to our way of seeing the world: permaculture, biodiversity and the ecological footprint.

Permaculture—permanent culture or permanent agriculture—is a comprehensive,

holistic means for planning gardens, farms or entire communities. It is both a philosophy and a practical code for design, mandating the use of the fewest possible resources to achieve the greatest possible gain, whether in our personal lives or in the larger task of saving the planet. On a farm, permaculture translates into having the kitchen garden next to the kitchen, and the nut trees and lowest-maintenance perennials at the other end of the property. Permaculture practitioners look at what the earth (or anything else, for that matter) has to offer and plan accordingly. Why drain a wet area when it could be used for a high-yield, high-value damp land crop like watercress, water chestnuts, cranberries or arrowroot? In the city, permaculturalists advocate the development of walking-distance neighbourhood shopping areas, with local food and specialty shops to discourage the building of big-box warehouses with large parking lots. On every conceivable scale, conserving energy opens opportunities for more creative use of time and natural resources.

The term *biodiversity* began to be widely used in conservation circles in the 1980s. It gave concrete expression to the notion that ecosystems are infinitely complex and interdependent. Species are eradicated routinely because humans have no material use for them, but biodiversity maintains that everything from a human appendix to a cockroach plays an essential role in the world, even if we do not yet know what that role is. For example, quite recently it came as a surprise to most foresters that the coastal rain forest needed "weed trees"—alder and birch—in order to survive. These "expendable" trees host microbes in the soil that maintain the health of cedars and hemlock. Biodiversity also supports the notion that the world is better off when power, wisdom and resources are shared rather than concentrated in the hands of a few.

The *ecological footprint* is a tool that can help us visualize human impact on the earth as well as aid us in measuring how much land is required to provide for the material needs of an individual—or a neighbourhood, a city, a country or a continent—for that entity's entire existence. North Americans consume more resources and create by far more waste than any other people in the world. If the North American standard of living were to be adopted elsewhere, it would require two and a half additional planets the size of Earth to support us. On the other hand, very positive results—nutritionally and environmentally—could be achieved if, for example, North Americans were to adopt a Mediterranean-style diet in which animal proteins are used mostly as a garnish and the consumption of fruits and vegetables is greatly increased.

Alice Waters, owner of the Chez Panisse Café and Restaurant in Berkeley, California, started a revolution of consciousness and taste in the mid-1970s when she demonstrated that a close connection between the land, the food preparer and the eater created healthier and happier people. We trust that reading this book will inspire you to join with others in your community (however you define it) to discover for yourself the pleasures of fresh, flavourful local food. You can nibble at this book whenever you please or devour it at a single sitting. Either way, we hope you will use it as a starting point to create your own delights.

Herb Barbolet

I. Growing

Something happens to people who **plant seeds**—it is impossible to watch a plant grow and flourish without getting a sense of the miracle of all life. Not so long ago, more than 50 per cent of the North American population lived on farms. Today, most of us live in urban settings. But our drive to grow things is still very strong, and the past fifteen years has seen a tremendous resurgence of interest in gardening. A stroll through many neighbourhoods takes you past small plots lush with vegetables and flowers. People without back yards or balconies may be inspired to have a windowsill herb garden, and those who can't do that might sprout alfalfa or mung beans in their kitchens. At the other end of the scale, the number of farmers with large commercial operations has steadily declined. As agriculture becomes concentrated in fewer and fewer corporate hands, there is a corresponding decrease in the variety, flavour and nutritional value of the food available to consumers.

Much of the food we buy today comes from Third World countries. Peasants whose ancestors tilled the earth to provide food for their families are now growing for export, forgoing the production of food for themselves in order to provide North Americans with coffee or oranges or bananas. With the money they earn, these growers are urged to buy pesticides or herbicides that will enable them to produce larger crops for sale, or to buy soft drinks or fast-food snacks to replace their local diets. By contrast, when we grow our own food, or buy food in season from local producers, everyone benefits.

An increasing number of people are demanding food that is not produced in a chemical soup, or blasted with radiation, or created by splicing genes in ways that nature never intended. Many of us also miss an earlier, less urban existence where we had a more direct connection to the earth. For some, growing food is a solitary activity, a chance for exercise and fresh air and a sense of working in conjunction with the natural world. For others, it is a team sport; in community gardens and on co-operative farms the land and the labour are shared, and in seed exchange programs people barter not only seeds but the wisdom of the ages. For still others, growing food commercially is the fulfillment of a long-held dream to escape the city. In this chapter, you'll meet all kinds of growers. Their stories may even prompt you to plant some seeds of your own.

—H.B.

5

Composting

Composting is the breaking down, or decomposition, of organic matter by microorganisms into nutrient-rich, sweet-smelling soil. Compost supplies the three main nutrients needed for plant growth—nitrogen, phosphorous and potassium—as well as trace elements seldom found in commercial soil. Humus, the final product, releases nutrients slowly for plants to take up through their roots and improves the structure of the soil.

Not all of us have the luxury of a back yard where we can let compost pile up. Commercial bins designed to keep compost neat, out of sight and pest-proof are available in all sizes and price ranges, from small plastic totes for worms to build-it-yourself wooden or mesh boxes. Visit your local compost demonstration garden and ask your composting friends for advice before deciding what system might suit you best.

Whatever your choice of container, the process is the same.
1. Start with a layer of coarse material: small branches pruned from trees, straw or grass clippings.
2. Add a layer of old compost, manure, garden soil and/or seaweed to start the action.
3. Alternate layers of green and brown: green (kitchen scraps) for nitrogen and brown (leaves) for carbon. Include vegetable trimmings, garden waste, hair, lawn clippings, coffee grounds and filters, tea bags, corn cobs (chop first), and crushed clam, oyster and egg shells. Avoid greasy food scraps, dairy products, meat and fish, since these things take a long time to break down and will attract pests. No to cat litter, charcoal briquettes and coal.
4. Keep each layer a maximum of 6" deep to prevent matting. Organic material decomposes faster if shredded into small pieces.
5. Mix every six to eight weeks. Expect finished compost in about four months. Unmixed, it will take about a year.

❦ Community Alternatives Co-operative

West Second Avenue is a typical Vancouver street—until you look a little more closely at one particular garden. A hedge of currant bushes, rosemary and roses separates beds of thyme, fennel, calendulas, tomatoes, beans, peppers, leafy salad greens and colourful flowers from the sidewalk. Finding land put to use like this is rare in an urban setting, and meeting the people who care for the garden reveals that they—and the place they live—are just as unusual.

In 1979, concerned about urban alienation and a disappearing sense of community, a group of social activists secured a contract with the Canada Mortgage and Housing Corporation to create a housing co-operative in Vancouver's Kitsilano neighbourhood. Except for the solar collectors on its roof, the four-storey cedar and glass building appears to be typical of its era. But wrapped around an airy courtyard, and designed to house people in shared living spaces, the Community Alternatives Co-operative can actually best be described as an urban village, with forty-one residents ranging in age from newborns to seniors.

Putting the grounds around the co-op to productive use was a major goal right from the start. Kaz Takahashi, one of the original

members, describes how viable land was hacked out of heavy clay hardpan in order to plant an edible landscape, an idea viewed at the time as distinctly eccentric. Then, as now, vegetable trimmings from co-op households were recycled to create rich food for the soil. "Beulah," a large motorized rotary composter painted black and white, is kept in the co-op's underground parking area. Inside Beulah, vegetable refuse is layered with leaves collected each fall from the neighbourhood. Perhaps because it is continually nourished, the garden gives back produce almost year-round: brassicas, rosemary and chervil can be picked in January.

Over the years, crops have changed according to individual preferences. Every spring, each person who wants to garden chooses a growing area. Members organize periodic work parties to maintain common pathways. The more enjoyable job of picking fruit and vegetables is also shared, as is the harvest.

Every square inch of garden space is utilized. To the west is a narrow area where plants salvaged from houses scheduled for demolition create a joyous tangle of foxgloves, fragrant sweet rocket, purple lunaria and papery red-orange Chinese lanterns. On the building's shady east side grow raspberry canes, patches of mache that reseed themselves from year to year, and a corkscrew willow that Takahashi cuts for ikebana arrangements.

Many plants are multipurpose. Rambling amiably over the front entrance, a Concord grapevine is a source of fruit, materials for decorative wreaths and refuge from the summer sun. Lemon balm and mint appear in tisanes and salads. Comfrey leaves can be strewn in a bath to soothe the skin, and the plant's flowers are edible. Pear, plum and apple trees provide fruit and a shady place to relax with a book and a mug of tea. Salad bar, florist, apothecary: the garden is all of these. Co-op children discover at an early age that the young feathery shoots of fennel are wonderfully sweet and the green seeds of sweet cicely taste like licorice.

Although the co-operative is a community unto itself, its residents are far from insular. Perhaps the most powerful bridge between Community Alternatives and the rest of the area is the living fence, which fosters neighbourliness. "Early on, passersby would stop and say, 'I haven't seen that since I was in Europe,'" Takahashi recalls, pointing to the red, black and white currants the hedge produces. "I'm often out here early in the morning picking off worms. That's when you see people going to work or taking the dog out, and kids going to school asking, 'What's that, Mommy?' Our hedge is a conversation piece. In the old days, they thought we were crazy. But now, more and more, the response is that of course we should use the land we have to grow whatever we can."

Compost, like all living things, needs oxygen, food and water in proper balance. To prevent your compost from becoming anaerobic (a condition in which putrid-smelling bacteria flourish), you will need to introduce air. Poke at the compost with a stick, broom handle or aerating tool. Turn it if you have room, and add a layer of soil or finished compost from the bottom of the heap.

Compost should be as moist as a wrung-out sponge. At under 40 per cent water content, compost will decompose too slowly; at over 60 per cent, the aerobic bacteria will drown. If your compost is too wet, dry it out by turning, fluffing, poking and adding dry material such as straw or shredded newspaper. Cover it with plastic in the rainy season. Poke holes in compost that is too dry and pour unsalted vegetable water in the holes.

Since over 30 per cent of our "garbage" is compostable, composting is an easy way to care for the planet. If you don't have a garden, give your compost to a gardener friend.

Stinging Nettles

Velma Barbolet, Fraser Common Farm

Stinging nettles are one of my favourite vegetables; they are so versatile. You can use them in any recipe that calls for spinach, and they are especially good in lasagna. Nettles mixed with sour cream, yoghurt or mayonnaise make a wonderful veggie dip. Chopped with garlic and other herbs, they become a sauce for rice, pasta or potatoes, and they can also be combined with parmesan cheese to make pesto.

Velma Barbolet harvests nettles, one of the first crops of spring.

❦ Fraser Common Farm

Fields, wildflowers and red barns line the rolling roads of British Columbia's Fraser Valley. Driving down one of them, you come to a small sign that reads "Fraser Common Farm Co-op." Further along a winding track are a barn and a farmhouse, with a solar greenhouse and a "salad shack" nearby. Stretching as far as the eye can see are rows and rows of herbs and greens bursting with health.

The genesis of the farm lies in the mid-1970s, when the Community Alternatives Society decided to create a rural community made up of clustered housing and cottage industries. The thirty-five people at the nucleus ranged in age from twenty to sixty and included a fisher, a carpenter, a teacher, an urban planner, a jewellery maker and an artist.

When initial plans to lease land came to nothing, the group decided to pool their capital and purchase property. Its benign climate and long tradition of farming made the Fraser Valley, to the east of Vancouver, especially attractive. The group secured a ten-acre family farm for $75,000 and incorporated it as a co-operative.

Despite the dream of country living, most co-op members still made their livings in the city, and most had no hands-on agricultural experience. So the original idea of a self-sustaining farm evolved into the concept of a rural-urban community. The farm would be a source of food and a place to retreat, relax and celebrate; urban housing at the Community Alternatives Co-op in Vancouver would let members continue their city jobs. People could enjoy the best of both worlds.

As it turned out, the group had purchased an exceptional piece of land. "It's a very long, narrow parcel with large, fairly mature stands of trees," says Herb Barbolet, one of the farm's original founders. "Water comes onto the property in five different places, and we have a spring that feeds water year-round. One of the streams has salmon spawning." Pheasants, deer and coyotes have all been spotted on the property.

At first, although thimbleberries, brambles, salmonberries and elderberries grew on the farm in profusion, the land was largely populated by thistles, buttercups, dandelions, wild mustards and nettles. In the early 1980s, the co-op hired an organic gardener to remedy the situation. The newly churned soil became a hospitable venue for seeds of any kind, and more wild plant varieties established themselves, a bright tapestry of johnny-jump-ups, chickweed, lamb's-quarters, shepherd's-purse, purslane and wild amaranth, as well as wild medicinal plants.

Over the years, plum, hazelnut and crab apple trees have been planted at the farm periodically, often to mark a birth or a passing among co-op members. An inspirational day at the farm for daycare workers and their charges often ends with a tree planting as well. Currant and raspberry bushes have slowly augmented the wild berry varieties, and commemorative plants, such as a rosebush for a sixtieth birthday, add to the profusion of colour.

As many as thirteen people lived at Fraser Common Farm in the original farmhouse and outbuildings; today, a new farmhouse is home to five residents. And for more than a decade the farm has also been the official home of the Glorious Garnish and Seasonal Salad Company, a venture that has played a central role in the evolution of B.C.'s thriving regional cuisine.

The Glorious Garnish and Seasonal Salad Company

For centuries, a "salad" meant a mix of many different greens and herbs. A six-hundred-year-old recipe for "salat" lists parsley, sage, garlic, onions, young onions, leeks, borage, mint, fennel, cresses, rue, rosemary and purslane among its ingredients. North American produce stores in the mid-eighties offered scant choice by comparison. Iceberg lettuce had become the staple for salads; romaine lettuce went straight into Caesar salads, and expensive imported endive showed up only in specialty stores. Those items apart, choice was virtually nonexistent. It was a vivid example of how drastically agribusiness had reduced the variety of foods available to consumers.

In 1985, Fraser Common Farm co-op members Herb Barbolet and

Nettles grow wild in swampy areas. When I worked at a daycare in a rural setting, I taught the children to identify the plants, and they would come running to me excitedly when they spotted some. I would get my harvesting glove and follow the nettle patrol to our destination. We would steam the nettles, then chop them up with a little salad dressing and have them on crackers for a snack.

Nettles have significant health benefits as well. When I was diagnosed with stage three breast cancer, I reluctantly agreed to undergo chemotherapy. One of the side effects of the drugs is that they really harden your veins. I read somewhere that drinking nettle tea would keep my veins healthy, so I religiously drank it every morning at breakfast time. When I went in for my seventh chemo treatment, the technician remarked on what good shape my veins were in. After chemo and a lot of complementary medicine and daily meditation, my surgery showed that I was completely clear of cancer.

I really look forward to the spring, when the new shoots of stinging nettle start popping up everywhere on the farm. You can use the whole plant until it is about a foot high, but I like to get to the plants when they have only four or five leaves. Picking these encourages new growth to appear.

Blanch nettles by placing them in boiling water for 90 seconds. The nettle water is full of nutrients and iron, and it's an excellent soup base. Chop cooled nettles coarsely and place in plastic bags in the freezer. Thaw as needed.

Making Your Own Celebration Salad

Celebrate the changing seasons by growing greens, herbs and edible flowers in your back yard, on your balcony or in hanging baskets. Remember that "greens" come in shades of red and white as well.

Red orach and magenta spreen planted in early spring will add many variations on red to your early summer salad. Ruby chard and bull's blood beet tops, planted in succession, ensure colour until the hard frost hits. Radicchio turns red as the days shorten, becoming crisp and bittersweet after the first frost. Kales, which range from light-green Siberian and dark blue-green Lacinato to purple and white Peacock and Chidori, are sweetest in the fall. With any luck, they will last all winter, and in the spring will give you crucifers (crunchy shoots) before they explode into a mass of edible yellow flowers. Garnish your salad just before serving as these flowers have a very short shelf life.

Fresh herbs are always a culinary adventure. Be bold. If you like the flavour of an herb, it will probably be wonderful in your salad. Most perennial herbs will grow again if cut back; use them as long as they are tender and tasty. Three plantings of annuals will ensure flavour from early summer to late fall. Early spring perennial salad herbs

Heather Pritchard were awarded a government grant to research ways that small land-owners could supplement their incomes. Their timing was opportune: culinary knowledge and interest were growing by leaps and bounds. In New York, a small gourmet store called the Silver Palate had added the word "arugula" to everyday vocabulary. In California, chefs like Jeremiah Tower and Alice Waters were spearheading the development of a regional cuisine based on seasonal, locally sourced ingredients.

Barbolet and Pritchard also knew of the mesclun of France and Italy's saladini, the mix of tiny flavourful greens that results when farmers and gardeners thin their seedlings. Their research involved a field trip to Pragtree Farm near Seattle, arguably the first farm in North America to sell wild and exotic greens to restaurants. Inspired by Pragtree's owner Marc Musik, Barbolet and Pritchard began to experiment with more than a hundred varieties, including herbs, edible flowers and five different kinds of mustard greens—among them mizuna, Osaka purple and green wave, varieties then almost unknown anywhere else in Canada.

Their product made its first appearance at Isadora's Co-operative Restaurant in Vancouver, where then-chef Hubertus Surm worked with the newly formed Glorious Garnish and Seasonal Salad Company to fine-tune the balance of ingredients. As customers quickly discovered, "greens" was a misnomer for the plate of yellow flowers and jewel-like purple, red, green and white leaves aptly dubbed "Celebration Salad."

But it was Vancouver's Expo 86 that catapulted the Glorious Garnish and Seasonal Salad Company into the culinary limelight. Pritchard, originally from the Northwest Territories, was hired to train the Territories' pavilion staff in urban survival skills. Spotting an opportunity, she contacted the pavilion restaurant's chef and suggested he sample their salad. Suddenly, the neophyte salad company found itself with an order of forty to eighty pounds of greens a week for the next six months.

There was just one problem: even if seeded right away, new plants wouldn't grow in time to meet the deadline. Ingenuity came to the fore. Members of the company scoured meadows and hedges for edible wild greens such as chickweed, sorrel, lamb's-quarters and dandelions. They scrounged ingredients from nearby farms. When a local organic farmer offered radishes, they composted them and added the leaves to the salad. Small beets were made into pickles; their greens went into the mix.

It paid off. Icicles, the N.W.T. pavilion's restaurant, was a major success at the fair. On the advice of Vancouver food writer and chef James Barber, Barbolet contacted other local chefs, who quickly recognized the customer-drawing potential of Celebration Salad. Pan Pacific Hotel chef Ernst Dorfler played an important role in the company's early success, as did noted chefs Kerry Sear of the Four Seasons and Lars Jorgensen at the William Tell.

By the summer of 1987, the Glorious Garnish and Seasonal Salad Company was supplying ten Lower Mainland restaurants; the following year that rose to twenty. A year later, close to 125 different food plants were growing at the farm, including experimental exotica such as yellow and purple snow peas. The company followed organic growing principles from the start, and in 1990 it was certified organic by the recently formed B.C. Association for Regenerative Agriculture.

Edible flowers became a company specialty. Since not all blooms can be eaten, Glorious Garnish wisely enlisted Sinclair Philip of Sooke Harbour House and Dr. Nancy Turner of the Royal British Columbia Museum as consultants. When the public's passion for edible flowers eventually waned, the company let cilantro plants go to seed, marketing the result as "green coriander," and sold the attractive flowering tips that conclude a brassica's life cycle as garnishes and salad ingredients.

Consistently in the vanguard of culinary exploration, and well aware of its pioneering role, Glorious Garnish has always happily shared its knowledge. It co-operates with universities, under-

include bronze fennel, chervil, lovage, lemon balm, mints, sweet cicely and sorrel. Buckler sorrel leaves are exactly the right size for a salad.

In summer and fall, try licorice-tasting anise hyssop, spicy purple ruffles basil and peppery nasturtium leaves in various colours. Plant arugula (rocket) frequently for a long season of spicy nuttiness. Use the tips and flowers as well.

Forage for wild seasonal greens to add to your home-grown or purchased ingredients. These appear wherever the soil is cultivated, and they are more nutritious and flavourful than many of the plants we carefully tend. Learn to identify the wild plants in your garden and add them generously to your seasonal salad mix. Some common varieties are chickweed (spring/fall); oxeye daisy leaves (spring); lamb's-quarters (summer); mallow (fall); mustard (spring/fall); pigweed (summer); purslane (summer); shepherd's-purse (spring/fall); sheep sorrel (summer); wood sorrel (summer); and wintercress (spring/fall).

Glorious Garnish and Seasonal Salad Company partners Susan Davidson (left), Dave McCandless and Heather Pritchard.

Edible Flowers

Edible flowers are a delicious and beautiful addition to salads and other fresh dishes. Grow your own or buy flowers that are certified organic; regular commercial flowers often contain harmful pesticides and herbicides.

Anise hyssop *(Agastache foeniculum)*: Sweet, purple, licorice-flavoured flowers.	July–September
Bachelor's buttons *(Centaurea cyanus)*: Use petals in salads and wedding cakes and as confetti.	July–early September
Borage *(Borago officinalis)*: Very fragile. Use immediately after harvesting.	July–early October
Brassicas—kales, broccoli, mustards *(Brassicas)*: Tatsoi and mizuna are superior.	April–October
Calendula/Pot marigold *(Calendula officinalis)*: Reseeds easily and, weather permitting, blooms year-round.	June–October
Carnations *(Dianthus)*: Depetal for salads.	July–September
Carnations, Pinks *(Dianthus caryophyllus)*: Use whole as decorations or depetal for salads.	July–September
Chervil *(Anthricus cerefolium)*: Harvest the whole flowering tip.	October–early November
Chives (garlic) *(Allium tuberoscum)*: Sprinkle florets into anything that needs a touch of garlic.	May–June
Chives (onion) *(Allium shoenoprasum)*: Sprinkle florets into anything that needs a touch of onion.	May–June
Comfrey *(Symphytum)*: Use the tip in salad, just as the purple begins to show.	April–May
Elderflowers *(Sambucus)*: Very short shelf life.	April–early May
Flowering currant *(Ribes sanguineum)*: Has a slight resin taste, so use sparingly.	April
Forget-me-nots *(Myosotis)*: For intense blue, try Chinese forget-me-nots *(Cynoglossum)*.	April
Johnny-jump-ups *(Viola tricolor)*: Minty flavour.	Volunteers year-round
Lilac *(Syringa)*: Use the tiny, bitter-tasting florets for a hint of colour.	April–May
Lung wort *(Pulmonaria)*: Blue and pink.	April
Mallow *(Malva sylvestris)*: Deep purple. Can withstand fall rains and light frost.	September–November
Marigold *(Tagetes)*: Very versatile. Depetal flowers for salads.	July–early September
Money plant/Silver dollar *(Lunaria)*: Whole flower can be eaten fresh. Bitter taste.	April–early May
Nasturtiums *(Tropaeolum majus)*: Extend the season by starting indoors.	Late June–September
Pea (vegetable) *(Pisum)*: Eat flowers of edible peas, not sweet peas *(Lathryus)*.	June–July
Pineapple sage *(Salvia elegans)*: Sweet red florets. Plant needs to be protected.	Mid-August–September
Primrose *(Primula vulgaris)*: Multicoloured.	April
Roses *(Rosa species)*: Vary in flavour. Some varieties will grow well into fall.	May–July
Sweet cicely *(Myrrhis odorata)*: Delicate, white, sweet, licorice-tasting flowers.	May–June
Sweet rocket *(Hesperis matronalis)*: Wildflower with fragrant white, pink and mauve florets.	April–May
Viola/Pansies *(Viola)*: Minty.	Can be grown year-round

takes research and offers a mentoring program. Tours of the farm are common. Visitors from the Smithsonian Institution, food writers from various countries, and biology and plant science students have all walked the narrow path from the barn to the upper meadow and across to the fields.

Today, run by Susan Davidson, Dave McCandless and Heather Pritchard, the Glorious Garnish and Seasonal Salad Company is the antithesis of monoculture—more like a multiculture, perhaps—growing a wide variety of crops in very small quantities. It is a labour-intensive process. Apart from the use of a dryer, picking, washing and packaging are all done by hand. Produce is shipped ready to use, and use it chefs do, often as a jumping-off point for creativity. Sushi master Tojo Hidekazu, for example, substitutes green wave mustard for the traditional nori in maki rolls served at his Vancouver restaurant, Tojo's.

In keeping with permaculture principles, waste remains on the farm to nurture the land. Fifty chickens are deliberately situated next to the compost heap, and soil is also enriched through crop rotation and through growing green "manures" such as rye, buckwheat, peas and fava beans. Only the tips of some plants are picked, so that much of the growing matter remains to feed the soil; "cut and come again" crops are popular for the same reason.

It has not always been smooth sailing. The company hit hard times in the 1990s when California businesses flooded the market with premixed salads priced well below local growers' production costs. But Glorious Garnish's owners regrouped, "revisioned," refinanced and broadened their customer base beyond gourmet restaurants. These days, you'll find glorious garnishes and seasonal salads for sale at farmers' markets as well.

True to their original goals, the people behind the Community Alternatives Co-op, Fraser Common Farm and the Glorious Garnish and Seasonal Salad Company continue to feed themselves—and others—with what grows in their own back yard.

JOHN BISHOP'S **SPICY CHERRY AND RED CURRANT SOUP**

John Bishop is regarded as the ultimate host by all who eat at his highly regarded Vancouver restaurant, Bishop's. He and his staff are fanatical about what goes into their dishes. "Ingredients are king—we look for quality and freshness," says Bishop. "We play with food the same way an artist plays with paints. We let the ingredients tell us what to cook. A supplier brings in a load of razor clams, and they become our evening special. Someone picks a bunch of elderberry blossoms from a tree growing wild, and their distinctive fragrance inspires a sauce."

1 lb./500 g Bing cherries, pitted
8 oz./250 g red currants
1 cup/250 mL orange juice
4 cups/1 L red wine OR raspberry or strawberry juice
2 sticks cinnamon
6 whole cloves
4 whole star anise
1 tsp./5 mL ground allspice
4 oz./125 g fresh basil
2 cups/500 mL carbonated mineral water

In a large bowl, combine all ingredients except mineral water. Allow to stand for 30 minutes to infuse flavours, then strain or pass through a food mill. Chill 1-2 hours. Add carbonated mineral water just before serving. *Serves 8.*

HUBERTUS SURM'S **WEST COAST SALAD WITH INDIAN CANDY**

"We were one of the first to put a focus on healthy food," says Hubertus Surm of the time when he was chef at Isadora's, the Vancouver restaurant he credits with introducing a distinctively West Coast approach to cuisine. German-born and -trained, Surm now lives on Saturna Island, where he is chef at a local lodge and partner in a general store.

VINAIGRETTE

1/4 cup/60 mL seasoned rice vinegar

1 tsp./5 mL chili paste

3 Tbsp./45 mL canola or light olive oil

SALAD

1 lb./500 g new potatoes

8 asparagus spears, blanched

1/2 lb./250 g mixed salad greens

4 strips Indian candy salmon, sliced

4 oz./125 g smoked sockeye salmon, sliced

1 tomato, quartered

In a small bowl combine rice vinegar and chili paste, then slowly whisk in oil. Set aside.

Wash potatoes and steam (skins on) for 20 minutes or until a knife easily pierces the flesh. Cool and cut into 1/4"/16 mm slices. Sprinkle a little vinaigrette over potatoes and reserve the remainder.

Arrange potato slices around the rim of a plate. Cut asparagus spears in half lengthwise and arrange on top of potatoes.

Toss salad greens with remaining vinaigrette and pile into middle of plate. Curl sockeye salmon into roses and place on top of salad. Arrange tomato wedges around rim of plate. Top with slices of Indian candy. *Serves 4.*

Chinese Greens
Stephen Wong

Need some variety in your life? The Chinese have been actively developing variety in their vegetables for thousands of years. In fact, for as long as anyone can remember, the word for vegetable—*tsai in* Mandarin and *choy* in Cantonese—has been a catch-all term that refers to everything eaten as an accompaniment to rice. Ancient members of the Brassica family, up to two hundred varieties at last count, have reportedly been cultivated since 5000 B.C.

Chinese greens have made a tremendous contribution to the Asian diet by augmenting the otherwise meagre food supply with minerals, vitamins and fibre. Now grown locally from B.C. to California, they are available all year round, and there's no excuse for not getting to know them better.

Cottonwood and Strathcona Gardens

Teacher and computer consultant Geoff McBeath swings a plastic bag of fruit and vegetable trimmings for his compost heap as he walks the six blocks from his East Vancouver apartment to Cottonwood, the urban communal garden where he grows vegetables. His route takes him past clothing outlets, paint factories and a set-building facility for Vancouver's thriving movie industry. Opposite one end of the garden is a large building housing a produce wholesaler. McBeath points out the irony of "trying to make your own agriculture with all these trucks rolling in from California." Vancouver land is among the most expensive in North America, which makes Cottonwood and neighbouring Strathcona Garden, which share six acres leased from the city, all the more remarkable. The site is a five-minute drive from the heart of downtown, a genuine urban oasis.

An organization called City Farmer received a federal Local Initiatives Project grant to start a Strathcona community garden here in 1985. At the time, the land was used only for industrial and commercial fill. Covered in broom bushes, the soil was virtually dead. Like adjacent Cottonwood Garden, then used for equipment storage, it belonged to the Vancouver Parks Board.

City Farmer was given a one-year lease for a fee of a dollar. A borrowed tractor was used to

level the ground, and community "rock picks" got rid of the worst of the landfill. "We virtually broke that land with no money and the poorest people in the neighbourhood," says Muggs Sigurgeirson, one of the original members of City Farmer. A donation funded the installation of a water line.

The local community was quick to appreciate the possibilities of their own neighbourhood garden, and by 1991 Strathcona had a long waiting list. More space was obviously needed. Today Cottonwood and Strathcona gardens are run by the nonprofit Strathcona Community Gardeners Society, and the initial one-year lease has been extended on a ten-year basis.

Cottonwood Garden provides space for a number of projects, among them a traditional First Nations sweat lodge shared by several groups from Vancouver's Downtown Eastside. "Four years ago, this was all blackberries," says Geoff McBeath of an area now claimed by the Environmental Youth Alliance, an organization whose focus is environmental education and activism. In late summer, corn grows tall, currant bushes glimmer with fruit, and renegade potatoes—a by-product of compost—flourish among the tomato plants. Bark-mulch pathways soften footsteps. The giant cottonwood trees that line the sides of the garden mute traffic noise to a dull rumble.

The membership of Strathcona and Cottonwood gardens is a real cross section, ranging from young families to seniors and representing a wide variety of professions and ethnic origins. Each member pays $10 to join the society and $15 a year for a plot. Lot sizes vary; 12' square is average. Some gardens are brilliant with edible flowers, others concentrate on herbs or vegetables. McBeath admits a personal preference for gardening defensively, deliberately growing species that are unusual in shape or colour as deterrents to theft. As examples, he indicates prickly looking lemon cucumbers and orange tomatoes that appear to be unripe even when they are ready to eat. When the tomatoes are finished, he will plant garlic. In the "winter" end of his garden are leeks, parsnips, beets and kale. Members tend their own plots, but there are also common areas, as well as a greenhouse, a garden shed and tools available for all to use. One Sunday a month, volunteers join forces to tackle such tasks as rebuilding paths and turning over the compost heaps.

Bok choy and its juvenile form, *baby bok choy*, are probably the best-known Chinese greens. The mature plant has thick, fleshy, milky-white stalks branching from a bulbous base. The leaves are dark green, shiny and slightly rumpled, with white veins running through them. Bok choy is great in stir-fries, and its mild flavour can also be enhanced by braising it in stock. When buying it, look for plants that are no taller than 8"or 9". Baby bok choy, generally sold in bulk, takes very little time to cook, so add it to your dish in the final stages of cooking for best results.

Bok choy sum, the flowering stalk of mature bok choy, is characterized by its round stem and clusters of yellow flowers and buds. It is sold in bundles and generally costs a bit more than bok choy, but it is more intense and sweeter in flavour. Stems with a small base (less than 3/4") are very tender when cooked. They are especially good in soups and stir-fries.

Shanghai bok choy, a close cousin of regular bok choy, has spoon-shaped leaves, thinner stalks and a lighter colour. Sold in bundles of four or five heads, it is at its best when no more than 5" to 6" tall. Its mild flavour, tender texture and brilliant colour make it the preferred garnish for many braised banquet dishes.

Bok choys are quite perishable and will lose their supple, delicate texture if stored for more than two or three days, loosely wrapped in plastic, in your refrigerator. Older leaves can be dried and stored for later use in long-simmered soups. Soups made with dried bok choy are supposed to have a cooling effect on the system and aid digestion.

Choy sum is sometimes called "yow choy" or "yow choy sum" to avoid confusing it with bok choy sum. Choy sum, which means "vegetable heart," is typically harvested just when it begins to develop its yellow flowers, and it can be identified by the uniformly bright green colour of its stems and flat, rounded leaves. Pick stems that are 8" to 10" in length and not much more than 1/2" in diameter. Stir-fries and soups both benefit from this pretty vegetable.

Gai lan, commonly known as Chinese broccoli, is one of my favourite vegetables. Its flavour is rich and almost nutty, with a light hint of bitterness, and its dull, waxy stems and leaves turn a most attractive deep green when cooked. When prepared al dente, gai lan has an engagingly crunchy texture. Look for stems that are between 1/3" and 3/4" in diameter and about 6" to 8" in length, with healthy-looking bud clusters and white flowers. As with choy sum, avoid stems that have visible white dots. Use gai lan in stir-fries, soups or anything else you can dream up, and be assured that you are eating one of the most nutritious vegetables in the world. It's reputed to be a good source of calcium, iron and vitamins A and C. Gai lan will keep for four or five days in a plastic bag in your refrigerator.

Siu choy and *Tientsin cabbage,* commonly known as napa cabbage and *wong nga bak,* are the staple greens of northern China. They travelled to Korea to become the famous and fiery kimchi, when pickled in brine and chilies, and to Japan as a staple in fire-pot dishes. They are deliciously sweet-tasting when braised or cooked in soups. Because of their size and tightly packed leaves, these cabbages can be kept for up to two weeks when refrigerated. Just discard any dry, wilted leaves on the outside and cook as desired.

Yin choy, or Chinese spinach, actually belongs to the amaranth family. It comes in several varieties, with fuzzy-textured leaves that range from pale to dark green; leaves have a characteristic red to purple tinge radiating from the centre. Prepare yin choy as you would spinach. My favourite way to eat it is stir-fried with a bit of butter and some chopped garlic.

Ong choy, or water spinach, is also not a spinach. It is pale green in colour with arrowlike leaves and long hollow stems. It is not distinctly flavourful on its own, but it has an interesting crunchy texture. Popularly stir-fried with shrimp sauce or fermented bean curd and garlic, it is rich in iron and minerals.

Tong ho choy, or chrysanthemum leaves, is specially cultivated. These lacy greens have a soft, spinachlike texture and are sold in bundles that may sometimes appear a bit wilted. As long as they are not dried out, they can be easily refreshed in cold water. These greens can be eaten in a salad or in stir-fries, but they are most popular as additions to soups in both Japanese and Chinese cooking. Tong ho choy is a staple in Chinese "hot pot" restaurants.

Cottonwood gardener Austin Yu displays a handful of beets grown in his urban plot.

Just off the main path is a small area where trees and shrubs ring a small pond: an Asian garden, in which many species are experimental. Capable of growing as much as 12' a year, an Empress tree (*Paulownia tomentosa*) has leaves as large as parasols. Sansho, a Japanese tree, is grown for its peppery pods and lemon-flavoured leaves. A paper mulberry has leaves that are deeply notched; each one looks like a Rorschach test. "We have a number of persimmons, too," says McBeath. "They're a bit dicey, so we're trying different varieties. And here's an Asian pear." Bamboos sigh in the wind, but they are more than merely decorative. The eventual plan is to excavate a trench around the bamboo clumps and harvest the edible shoots that pop up from their bases in the spring.

Dug by hand, the pond in the Asian garden is lined with bentonite and sand, which together form an impermeable lining when wet; it attracts a variety of birds, among them American goldfinches, bushtits and, once in a while, red-tailed hawks. Juan Lake, another hand-dug pond within Cottonwood Garden, has developed its own ecosystem and even provided a temporary home for nesting ducks.

Austin Yu, originally from southern China, has been gardening at Cottonwood since 1991. The white picket fence of his plot can barely restrain the profusion of greenery inside. Yu grows intensively, as is traditional in China, using every possible inch of space. The pathways between his beds are a narrow, but still functional, one plank wide. The thick stems of hairy melon plants have been encouraged to twine vertically up bamboo supports and across lattice, from which melons

hang like heavy lanterns. Massive pendulous squash, striped yellow and green, can be seen through the leafy vines that ramble along his back fence. "I don't know the English name," says Yu, who has many of the seeds sent to him from China.

Yu comes twice a day to his garden, in the morning to plant, harvest and tie up, and in the evening to water. The earth in his plot is so fertile it's almost black, fed by compost and the soy bean by-products that Yu obtains from a nearby tofu factory. "Very rich when rotten," he smiles.

In one section of a bed, a plastic liner retains moisture, allowing watercress to flourish. Yu is also trying out American ginseng plants for the first time. He explains that his orange-red wolfberries are good for the eyes and that purple-green shiso leaves can be used both in fish dishes and to ward off colds. He may even have developed a new vegetable. His attempts to grow authentic Chinese long beans failed: "They gave flowers but the beans very, very tiny." Bees pollinated other varieties, however, and what has resulted is a new bean, half-Chinese and half–North American. It would be difficult to think of a more fitting symbol for these thriving community gardens.

STEPHEN WONG'S **GAI LAN WITH OYSTER SAUCE**

Hong Kong–born chef, restaurant consultant and writer, Stephen Wong has done more than anyone else in Vancouver to reveal the secrets of Asian food to a non-Asian audience. His ground-breaking creativity has enhanced the reputations of many B.C. restaurants and been showcased in a number of cookbooks.

1 lb./500 g gai lan, washed and trimmed
3 cups/750 mL chicken stock
1/2 tsp./2 mL sugar
2 slices ginger
1 Tbsp./15 mL vegetable oil
1 Tbsp./15 mL sesame oil
3 Tbsp./45 mL oyster sauce

Trim ends of gai lan and cut any thick stems in half lengthwise.

In a wok, bring chicken stock, sugar and ginger slices to a boil over high heat. Add gai lan to stock and cook, covered, for 2-3 minutes or until just tender.

Strain stock and retain for other use, discarding ginger. Transfer gai lan to cutting board and cut into 3"/8 cm pieces.

In the wok, combine vegetable oil and sesame oil over medium heat until hot. Add cooked gai lan and toss to coat with oil, about 30 seconds. Arrange gai lan on serving platter, drizzle with oyster sauce and serve immediately. *Serves 4.*

❦ Salt Spring Seeds

Mansell Farm on Salt Spring Island is a lovely place to be on a summer day, with its brilliant blue cornflowers, silky scarlet poppies, pink echinacea blossoms, and orange and gold calendulas as flamboyant as an emperor's train. From a hundred feet away, the thickets of peas and beans and tidy rows of lettuces are also a sight that would make

The dried beans Dan Jason shells at his farm on Salt Spring Island will end up in gardens around the world.

any gardener's heart swell, but a closer look at these otherwise well-tended beds reveals something quite unexpected. The lettuces have grown tall and spindly. Pea bushes, their crop unpicked, have withered and dried to a uniform papery brown. These are not exceptions. Owner Dan Jason deliberately allows all he grows to reach the final stage of its natural cycle—because seed is his business.

Through his company, Salt Spring Seeds, Jason sells his product by mail all across North America and as far afield as New Zealand, Australia, Africa and Europe. A profound love of gardening and an equally profound appreciation for food mean that Jason doesn't offer all the seed varieties commonly found in garden centres. He concentrates instead on high-protein, good-tasting and high-yielding crops—"beans, vegetables and herbs that contribute to self-reliance," as he writes in his catalogue, which also provides information on things like how to thresh wheat at home. "I strongly believe that everyone should have access to a healthy diet," says Jason, and his goal is to free his customers from dependence on store-bought, imported and out-of-season produce.

Plants, as Jason points out, are tremendously flexible in their uses. He mentions thatched-roof cottages and the bamboo scaffolding that climbs thirty storeys in Hong Kong as examples. Most of the plants he sells are certainly multi-taskers. Amaranth has spectacular flowers, leaves that can be eaten raw or cooked, and seeds that can be simmered to make a protein-rich dish.

In a society accustomed to thinking that tomatoes are red and beans are green, Jason's selection is an eye-opener. There are seeds from Tigerella tomatoes striped reddish-orange and gold, as well as from the yellow-and-green Green Zebra, the bright-yellow Taxi variety and Black Krim, with its dark-brown skin and flesh. His list of bush beans includes evocative names such as Dragon Tongue, Scarlet Bees, Limelight and Molasses Face. A garlic data base compares the flavour, number of cloves and keeping quality of fifty-two different varieties. His seeds come from all over the world, and among the less familiar names in his catalogue are Ashwaganda, a medicinal root from India; the intensely blue Anchusa, whose blossoms can be added to salads; and Cressonnette Marocaine lettuce, with its dramatic red and green colouring.

Growing things have always held a fascination for Dan Jason. In 1969 he wrote a book called *Some Useful Wild Plants*. A few years later, while working at a local yoga and meditation centre with a mandate to grow as much food as possible, he started experimenting with high-protein crops such as amaranth, soybeans and quinoa. "My whole progression was one of amazing discovery," says Jason. "I didn't understand why more people weren't growing these things." Many of the grains he discovered were grown from heritage seeds, some going

Collecting Your Own Seed

For centuries, people have collected seeds from their healthiest and most desirable plants, stored them in a cool, dry place and planted them again in the spring. This natural selection, passed down through generations, ensures that varieties well suited to local growing conditions are preserved and introduces new ones. If you are growing plants that are fertile, you too can collect your own seeds. You might want to tag specific plants with brightly coloured markers to remind yourself to save the seed.

Beans
Beans are a wonderful seed for the beginning gardener to collect. Allow pods to dry on a mature plant until they rattle. (If it starts to rain before pods are completely dry, harvest them and lay them out on a screen indoors to finish the process.) Pick off dried pods and stamp on them to release the seeds. Place seeds in a clearly labelled plastic container and store in a cool, dry place. The fridge works fine.

Tomatoes
Select a handful of ripe tomatoes. Put them in a plastic container, mush them by hand or with a masher, and allow them to ferment for about three days. Then spray mush with water, using either a garden hose or a strong stream from the kitchen tap. Rub seeds away from the pulp as you do this, and the viable seed will sink to the bottom of the container. Carefully pour off water and flesh. Then pour the remaining contents of the container through a screen. Leave seeds to dry on the screen in a hot, airy place for three to four hours, or until obviously dry. Place seeds in an envelope labelled with the name of the variety and date collected. Store in a sealed container in a cool, dry place.

back centuries; Black Einkorn, for example, is a type of wheat said to be ten thousand years old.

In 1987, Jason started his own farm. Keen to tell fellow gardeners about his discoveries, he produced a one-page listing that has expanded over the years as more and more varieties came to his attention. Plants on his two and a half acres are grown under organic growing principles, without herbicides, pesticides or synthetic fertilizers. Instead, Jason practises cover cropping, mulches, and spreads his gardens with manure from the llamas next door.

While he harvests enough to feed his extended family (as he points out, an acre of land can feed four to six people), most of Jason's crop is encouraged to go to seed. Collecting it is a labour-intensive process, as every species calls for different treatment. Often it is simply a matter of cutting a plant, or of bending it and rubbing the seed head between your hands, in both cases over a bucket. Chaff—plant debris and flower heads—must be sifted off with a screen, sometimes using a series of progressively finer meshes. Flowers can present a challenge, but even with their identifying petals long gone, Jason has trained his eye to distinguish the small seeds of sweet-smelling mignonette from those of Lemon or Tangerine Gem marigolds.

Although peak seed harvesting season is between July and October, lettuce and brassicas are sometimes left to grow right through the winter, so that they have a chance to produce flowers and seeds.

As Jason points out, "vast, amazing life" goes on within every seed head. Beetles, spiders and bugs love to take up residence in this moist, dark, food-filled world, but Jason puts a stop to that by leaving seeds in the sun to dry out. As a further precaution, seeds are placed in airtight plastic containers and left in a seed room all winter long to freeze. In January, Jason begins to parcel them into packets made from recycled paper, on which the growing instructions are printed in his signature green ink.

At Salt Spring Seeds, the relationship between seller and buyer is a close one. A letter from an overseas customer may include a new type of seed, and often the family story behind it. Jason tests every new variety he is given to see how easily it will grow and how it affects his tastebuds. If it meets his standards, he may add it to a subsequent catalogue. Gardeners frequently send him notes and comments on the prowess of a particular seed, information Jason enters into his data base.

Jason is always on the lookout for genetic throwbacks or chance crosses between breeds that can create other varieties: a purple chick bean; a snap bean with a vivid pink pod. "I'm working on that snap bean now," he says. "Hopefully, it'll stay true to its colour." The more new varieties of vegetables, grains and flowers around the better, in Jason's view; biodiversity is an important aspect of his work. As he digs in one of his gardens, his farm hums with life, summertime crickets and bees creating a constant symphony. "So many bugs, butterflies and birds come here," he says happily. "Word's got around."

DAN JASON'S **FAVA BEAN STEW**

Fava beans, which contain 30 per cent protein, are high in carbohydrates but low in fat. Their hardiness and high yields make them an ideal crop for coastal gardens. Soak dried beans overnight and then cook for one hour.

1/4 cup/60 mL butter or oil
1 large onion, chopped
1/2 cup/125 mL grated carrots
1 stalk celery, chopped
2 cloves garlic, minced
1/2 cup/125 mL all-purpose flour
1/4 tsp./1 mL dried thyme
salt and pepper to taste
pinch nutmeg
1 cup/250 mL vegetable stock
2 eggs, well beaten
1/2 cup/125 mL fresh French sorrel
1/2 cup/125 mL kale, chopped fine
4 cups/1 L cooked fava beans

Place a non-stick frying pan over high heat for 30 seconds and then add butter, onion, carrots, celery and garlic. Sauté for 5-8 minutes or until vegetables begin to soften.

Stir in flour, thyme, salt, pepper and nutmeg. Reduce heat to medium and cook gently for 1-2 minutes. Gradually add stock and simmer, stirring gently, for 10 minutes.

Reduce heat to low and stir in eggs slowly. Cook until eggs begin to set, about 1-2 minutes, and then stir in sorrel, kale and cooked fava beans. Heat through for 1-2 minutes and serve. *Serves 5-6.*

❦ Engeler Farm

As urban stress increasingly takes its toll, the dream of dropping out and finding a simpler life in the country is a popular one. For most, it remains just a pie-in-the-sky fantasy. But for one former Toronto couple who farm a five-and-a-half acre spread on southern Vancouver Island, it has become a reality.

Chef Mara Jernigan and wine expert Alfons Obererlacher trace the roots of their venture to the time they spent on sabbatical on Obererlacher's family farm in Austria. There, they saw how time-honoured farming traditions continued. There, Jernigan learned old-fashioned skills from her mother-in-law: plucking a chicken was one of them. There, too, their son Julian was born.

As a chef, Vancouver Island farmer Mara Jernigan appreciates the glorious flavours of home-grown produce.

The couple returned to Toronto, worked for a while, then moved west to Vancouver, where the idea of buying their own farm slowly blossomed into a concrete plan. Every weekend was spent leafing through real estate listings and following hand-drawn maps to out-of-the-way locations. Then, in May 1996, Jernigan heard that a small farm on Cobble Hill in B.C.'s Cowichan Valley was up for sale. The price was right; the terrain sounded promising. As she tells the story, she pulled into the driveway, eyed the land, saw its promise and said, "It's perfect." But the couple's circumstances definitely weren't. Jernigan was out of work, Obererlacher was employed as a waiter, their house in Toronto remained unsold and, most ominous of all, another potential buyer had already made an offer. Undaunted, Jernigan topped the offer, and when she got home Obererlacher too had important news: someone wanted to buy their Toronto property.

The couple named their new home Engeler Farm—farm of the angels. And indeed, its wraparound view of rolling green fields and chickens pecking contentedly under the plum trees makes it any urbanite's dream. But the cheerfully painted rooms of the seventy-year-old farmhouse and the orderliness of the garden around it belie the backbreaking labour required to work the transformation. While structurally sound, the house needed major cosmetic work throughout. The land required starting from scratch. But in return for sixteen-hour days, the couple found unexpected pleasures: floors of first-growth fir under the layers of gluey varnish and a wall of brambles that, when whacked away, revealed a Japanese garden complete with ponds and bridges.

Spending a few contemplative moments there is only a very occasional respite. Jernigan and Obererlacher's main project these days is the south-facing vineyard whose clay soil sucks up the heat and will, they hope, reward them with exceptional fruit. The first year, they planted Pinot Noir and Pinot Gris varieties, with most of their vine cuttings originating from the highly rated Blue Mountain vineyard in B.C.'s Okanagan Valley. The following year, wires went up to support the growing vines. A 6' fence protects the tender growth from deer and rabbits. There is no irrigation. "They're never going to get a drop of water from me," says Obererlacher, who knows that the harder a vine must claw into the soil for moisture, the more interesting its character.

Growing grapes is a matter of patience. It will be three years before their vines produce an initial crop; another two before they are in full production, generating an anticipated three and a half tons of grapes a year. Fortunately, other crops provide speedier results. Jernigan has put her culinary expertise to good use, knowing that the arduous work of planting and caring for specialty items like the one hundred gold raspberry canes that line the driveway will pay off in a ready market among gourmet restaurants.

Measuring 20' x 30', their vegetable garden is Jernigan's first—and her first season taught her that she had been over-enthusiastic, planting tomatoes too close together and strewing arugula seeds with such a liberal hand that the cullings filled a wheelbarrow. These vegetable trimmings are dinner for the farm's three resident pigs. As the couple

learned in Austria, the meat that results from animals fed on fresh produce and herbs is exceptionally flavourful. Jernigan raises Muscovy ducks, too, aware that they are eagerly sought by chefs. And of course the chickens keep the family supplied with fresh eggs.

Experience has taught Jernigan and Obererlacher that everything on a farm is a long-term project. A case in point: Jernigan was keen to make her own prosciutto. The technique was straightforward, if painstaking. Four pounds of salt were massaged into a whole raw ham, which was left to cure for a month in the farm's basement. Next, the ham was suspended by a loop of butcher's twine and hung outdoors on the sun porch. Some time later, a neighbour came over to perform the traditional test, using a sharp sliver of horse bone to check that the meat had not rotted inside. For its final aging, the ham was taken to a local butcher, who hung it in his walk-in freezer. It was almost a year before Jernigan, Obererlacher and friends were able to sample the prosciutto for the first time. The consensus? The work had been worth it.

Time, energy, passion: all are essential if you are bent on perfection, but forget farming if you are aiming for financial success, says Jernigan. The couple have become experts at making ends meet. The vineyard's fence posts of first-growth cedar were salvaged from a local forest company. Jernigan does consulting, teaches cooking classes and still cooks two nights a week at a local restaurant (from which she brings home pig slop, for a saving of $200 to $300 over the life of each animal). On a typical day, Obererlacher might Rototill a half-acre between the vines, help move 1,500 hay bales at a neighbouring farm (bartering his time for the use of a tractor), and go off to work as a waiter until one in the morning. Country ethics mean helping your neighbour: fifteen volunteers toiled side by side with the couple to plant the 1,000 vines that now grow in the vineyard.

Jernigan and Obererlacher's most creative venture so far is a series of events that let city-dwellers enjoy regional cuisine in a farm setting. Their first spring at the farm, they hosted a herb-planting class and a four-course dinner, and a fall event was marked by a full day of foraging for wild mushrooms. They have even turned what many would view as a drawback into a money-spinner. One night when the moon was full, with an expert on hand, they hosted a bat-watching party, where attendees were able to witness the nightly exodus of the six hundred residents of the farm's attic (where plastic sheeting collects their manure for use in the garden).

As they learn its natural rhythms, Jernigan and Obererlacher talk of responsible "stewardship" rather than ownership of the land. Permaculture is one of their guidelines; the dry summer climate inspired them to plant low-maintenance nut and fruit trees. Jernigan plans to teach chefs in training how to take a pig and use every part of it. A farm apprenticeship program is also in the works.

With fresh vegetables and herbs literally on her doorstep, Jernigan notes that her cooking has become far simpler. She is developing a repertoire of recipes using only what is obtainable on Engeler Farm, and dreams of creating an identifiable cuisine.

"I want our five and a half acres to be an example of how much you can do," says Jernigan. "Most of farming is just common sense. If you want to grow stuff, you need manure. If you want manure, you need a few animals. It's all part of keeping that balance. Sustainability is completely natural."

MARA JERNIGAN'S **PLUM CLAFOUTIS**

This French farmhouse dessert from the Limoges region is classically made with cherries but easily adapted to whatever fruit is in seasonal abundance: plums, apricots, peaches or pears. Clafoutis is great for breakfast or brunch. Serve with vanilla ice cream or whipped cream for a comforting dessert.

1/4 cup/60 mL melted butter, divided into 2 portions
1/4 cup/60 mL granulated white sugar
2 cups/500 mL small red plums, pitted
1/4 tsp./1 mL ground cinnamon
3/4 cup/180 mL almonds, sliced
4 eggs
3/4 cup/180 mL granulated white sugar
2 cups/500 mL whipping cream
3/4 cup/180 mL all-purpose flour
icing sugar to dust

Preheat oven to 350°F/180°C.

Brush the inside of a seamless 10"/25 cm cake pan with half the melted butter. Pour sugar into pan, coating bottom and sides. Shake excess sugar into a large mixing bowl. Add cinnamon to sugar and reserve. Spread almonds on bottom of pan and set aside.

Halve pitted plums, add to cinnamon sugar and toss to coat. Place plums in pan, skin side down, on top of almonds. Arrange a spiral pattern from the centre to cover entire pan.

In a mixing bowl, whisk eggs together, gradually adding 3/4 cup/ 180 mL sugar. Beat well and slowly add cream. Sift flour into mixture and whisk until well mixed. Stir in remaining melted butter. Pour batter over plums and transfer to hot oven. Reduce heat to 325°F/160°C after 10 minutes.

Bake for an additional 35-40 minutes. A toothpick inserted in the centre will come out clean when clafoutis is ready.

Cool on a rack for 10 minutes, cutting along edges of pan to free the pudding. Invert on a plate and serve warm or at room temperature with a liberal dusting of icing sugar. *Serves 6-8.*

❦ Townline Greenhouses

Karl Hann harvests crisp bell peppers in his organic greenhouse. A crop of melons hangs overhead.

Inside Karl Hann's greenhouse, it's a jungle. Literally. Pepper plants snake up long strings attached to the ceiling. Tomato plants—a dozen different varieties—bow under the weight of their fruit. His thirty banana trees, their ribbed leaves as large as a baby's cradle, are flourishing, as is the 12' papaya tree. Hann's intensely flavoured alpine strawberries are promising their highest yield ever. In his view, growing a single crop year in and year out is a boring way to make a living.

Hann left his native Romania for Canada in the 1970s. In 1992, along with a partner, he acquired an eight-acre property about a half mile from the Canada–U.S. border in B.C.'s Fraser Valley. He planted only long English cucumbers. The first year they rewarded his efforts with low returns, but he hung in, knowing all the time that what he really wanted to grow was specialty crops. Cucumbers, maybe, but a specific type of small cucumber favoured by the Asian market.

Hann admits he found it a challenge dealing with marketing boards, which required him to grow specific varieties of vegetables. "I decided I wanted to supply specialty markets and be my own marketer," he says. "It's quite different being independent. You have to set prices, find outlets, figure out how many peppers are going to be consumed."

In Hann's greenhouses, each 220' long by 120' wide, the atmosphere is warm, green

Good Soil

One of the most important factors in producing superior flavour is good-quality soil. Back-yard or organically grown vegetables taste better because their soil is richer. Crop rotation and composting ensure that nitrogen, phosphorus and potassium, along with some magnesium and micronutrients, are available for plant growth. Even if you are gardening in a small space, you can choose plants that will enhance your soil. For example, peas planted in early September will help replace nitrogen. Austrian winter peas will overwinter and give you an early crop of pea tips and edible purple flowers as well.

The best soil will hold together if squeezed and is not too slimy or porous. Although there are many commercial products ready-mixed for your gardening needs, it is not difficult to mix your own. A 14-part soil mixture might ideally include 7 parts compost; 3 parts peat moss; 3 parts vermiculite or perlite; and 1 part sand.

Soil that has too much clay or peat moss does not drain well. Soil that is too sandy drains too quickly and will not hold water. Ideally, you want a balance.

If soil is too heavy and drains poorly, add sand or perlite. If it's too light, add peat moss. Adding compost binds the iron in the soil and prevents it from being taken up by plants. A dose of fish fertilizer once a month should prevent nutrients from leaching out during heavy rainfall.

If you are worried about the health of your soil, you can have it tested. A commercial lab will analyze it for pH and a range of nutrients, and they will advise you about what to add for maximum growth potential. You can also buy a soil-testing kit at most nurseries.

UMBERTO MENGHI'S
ROASTED BELL PEPPERS

Say the name "Umberto" to anyone who relishes eating out and he or she will tell you of meals that capture all the spirit and colour of Tuscany. Opened in 1968, Menghi's first Vancouver restaurant, called Umberto's, was the prelude to a series of dazzling eateries. This ebullient restaurateur seeks out the intense flavours of seasonal fruits and vegetables, treating them with simplicity and respect.

Roasted peppers can be served as an antipasto, a garnish or an accompaniment to meat dishes. Choose peppers that are firm, heavy and unwrinkled.

Using a pair of long-handled tongs, place one pepper at a time in the open flame of a gas burner. Turn peppers occasionally while allowing them to become blistered and completely blackened. If you do not have a gas stove, arrange peppers on a broiler pan or on a hot charcoal grill, 3"/7 cm from the heat. Broil until entire surface of each pepper is charred.

When peppers are done, place them in a plastic bag, closing the bag after adding each one. Allow peppers to steam inside for 5-8 minutes. Rinse away blackened skins from peppers under cold running water. Cut in half and remove stems and seeds. Drizzle with a little olive oil and store, tightly sealed, in the refrigerator.

and fertile. As he originally intended, he now raises mini cucumbers. He grows ten different varieties of hot peppers, and his bell peppers are a riot of colour: red, green, yellow, purple, lilac and chocolate. Taut-skinned and glossy, they are heavier and juicier than those a consumer is used to finding in a supermarket.

Not that Hann sells to the major chains. Instead, he makes his produce available to organic stores, farmers' markets and restaurants, places where people appreciate the hard work he puts into maintaining quality. Meeting his customers face to face revealed their enthusiasm for vegetables that were naturally grown. So Hann switched to organic growing practices. "Before that, I used what everybody else used. I grew in bags filled with sawdust and dripped fertilizer in to get production." His plants today have their roots in soil and are fed on a diet of pig manure, fish fertilizer, seaweed and water.

He has also given up pesticide use. His papaya and banana trees and castor oil plants are not grown just for fun; they also provide shelter for bugs. Good bugs, Hann is swift to add, biological controls that keep other bugs away. Among them are encarsias, predator wasps that lay their eggs in the pupae of whiteflies; ladybugs quick to make a meal of aphids; and green and brown lacewings, which feed on insect eggs and pupae. He could use soap and oil sprays but prefers not to, knowing that they are nonselective.

A hummingbird feeder hangs from the roof. A monarch butterfly settles leisurely on Hann's shoulder. "If I had chemical sprays, I would never have butterflies, spiders or cobwebs," he says. "It is not easy to grow food this way. And chemical methods are less costly." He pauses to emphasize his point. "But you do not know what the long-term costs are." For Karl Hann, that makes all the difference.

JULIO GONZALEZ PERINI'S **POACHED TOMATOES WITH FRESH PEA SAUCE**

An Italian heritage and an Argentinian upbringing have given Villa del Lupo chef Julio Gonzalez Perini a passion for fine food. Training in Buenos Aires and stints at hotels and restaurants in Europe and across Canada have left him with a profound enthusiasm for simple but intense flavours. "I tend to use all fresh ingredients," he says, "only frozen if absolutely necessary, and always fresh herbs. In the late 1970s, I had a herb garden at my home. I used to grow fresh basil and take it to wherever I worked."

8-12 vine-ripened Italian tomatoes
$^1/_2$ cup/125 mL fresh peas, shelled
$^1/_4$ cup/60 mL pea shells, chopped
$^1/_4$ cup/60 mL chicken stock
2 Tbsp./30 mL olive oil
2 Tbsp./30 mL grapeseed oil
salt and pepper to taste

Bring a large pot of salted water to a boil. Cut tops off tomatoes. Plunge into boiling water for 1 minute, remove and cool at room temperature. Carefully remove skins and core tomatoes. Set aside.

Return salted water to a boil and add shelled peas for 1 minute. Remove and cool in ice water. Drain and set aside. Repeat with pea shells, cooking for 5 minutes. Chill shells in ice water.

Place pea shells in a blender and pour in half the chicken stock. Blend for 2-3 minutes, until smooth. Pass through a fine mesh strainer.

Add half the peas to the blender, along with remaining stock. Blend until smooth. Add pea shell purée, olive oil and grapeseed oil and process until smooth. Season with salt and pepper.

Warm tomatoes for 1-2 minutes in a 325˚F/160˚C oven and season lightly with salt and pepper. Place a mound of peas on the centre of each plate, top with pea sauce and place 2 or 3 tomatoes on each mound. *Serves 4.*

❦ Annie's Orchard

A Spartan eaten fresh from the tree is an apple at its best, so crisp you can hear yourself bite into it, its juices sweet and tart at the same time. Sadly, most apples aren't like that today. Bred for looks rather than flavour, their texture at its worst can be like polystyrene, and their taste a faint shadow of what it should be. A typical supermarket sells about six varieties of apples; Annie's Orchard, in B.C.'s Fraser Valley, has close to forty. Mary Ann and Jim Rahe moved to the farm in 1979, and their first apple tree went into the ground soon after. Trained as a plant pathologist, Jim, who works in the Biological Sciences department of Simon Fraser University, was curious to see what would grow on the couple's seven-acre spread. What

Mary Ann and Jim Rahe with a selection of newly propagated apple trees.

began as a hobby blossomed into a passion, and half the land is now given over to apple trees. "At the height of insanity, we had 254 named varieties," says Jim, but a less than ideal climate—"We're hammered with fungus disease"—forced them to whittle the number down to 30 or 40 main varieties, plus single trees of others. For purposes of comparison, Jim notes that Britain currently has a repository of no fewer than 3,000 kinds of apples.

Why so few types are sold in grocery stores is no mystery, says Jim. To succeed commercially, an apple must be attractive, resistant to bruising, capable of being stored for a year or more, and a variety that produces every year without fail. "When you're selling right off the farm," he says, "life span isn't quite so important."

Fall is definitely the big selling season at Annie's Orchard, where apple enthusiasts purchase by the pound or the box in the apple-stencilled "store" that occupies half the garage.

Which varieties are for sale depends on the month. Early producers like Transparent, a greenish-yellow apple that gets yellower as it ripens, and Starks Earliest, technically a cooking apple but also appealing to those who like a bit of snappy tartness, are picked in August. An excellent crop of juicy Gravensteins is usually ready about the first week of September. Prima or Dayton varieties and John Downie crab apples may also be available. A little later in September the Bramley crop should be ripe. This is the time too for the Rosu du Cluj to ripen, a Romanian apple whose flavour gets better the longer you keep it.

Even the most ardent apple lover will find some varieties that are completely unfamiliar. Jackie (named after a friend of the Rahes) originated at one of the breeding universities in the midwest U.S. ("They don't give them names," explains Mary Ann.) The E. B. Williams variety is available in early to mid-October. "It has an outstanding flavour, but a lot of russeting on the surface," says Jim. "Then again," adds Mary Ann, "people come here for an apple's flavour, not its appearance."

Jim himself has tried to add to the apple gene bank, a process that starts with evaluating different types of fruit that will meet the objectives he's set. He compares it to "looking at two parents and trying to guess what their kids will look like." Creating a new apple involves collecting seeds, growing seedlings and then grafting their buds on to root stock. It takes years—and it isn't always successful. "I've thrown away several," comments Jim ruefully. "They tasted terrible."

But nothing tempers the Rahes' enthusiasm for their favourite fruit. "It's a forgiving type of plant—you can make a mistake, and it will still survive. Some people like roses," says Jim. "I like apples."

ROBERT LECROM'S **ROASTED BUTTERNUT SQUASH, APPLE AND CIDER SOUP**

Growing up in Brittany exposed Hotel Vancouver executive chef Robert LeCrom to the vitality that fresh ingredients add to dishes. He treats his ingredients simply, whether he's working with luscious chanterelles or tasty Fraser Valley–grown spinach or tomatoes. "The demand for fresh local produce is there," says LeCrom. "If we push, the farmers will grow it."

3/4 lb./375 g butternut squash, peeled and cubed
1 Tbsp./15 mL butter
6 shallots, sliced thinly
2 cloves garlic, sliced thinly
3 green apples, cored, peeled and cubed
1 cup/250 mL sweet apple cider
2 cups/500 mL vegetable stock (or chicken if preferred)
1 cup/250 mL cream

Preheat oven to 400°F/200°C.

Bake squash for about 10 minutes, or until golden brown.

Heat a skillet over medium-high heat, and add butter, garlic and shallots. Sauté until moisture is evaporated. Add squash and apple. Cook for 2-3 minutes. Add cider and continue cooking. When liquid is almost evaporated, add stock and cook until ingredients are tender.

Add cream to skillet and bring to a boil. Boil until all ingredients are soft. Remove from heat. Transfer to blender or food processor and purée. Season with salt and pepper. Reheat in pot and serve. *Serves 4.*

❦ Ravenhill Farm

Like living calligraphy against the sky, ravens swoop and dive above Vancouver Island's Saanich Peninsula. At one particular stand of oak, arbutus and fir trees, a pot-pourri of fragrance drifts up to meet them, a heady mélange of fresh peppermint, pungent basil and the clean-linen smell of lavender—all of it part of the herbal abundance of Ravenhill Farm.

Today, when shoppers need go only as far as their local supermarket for fresh supplies of basil, dill or thyme, and every home cook knows the diffence between French tarragon (good) and the Russian variety (undesirable), it's hard to recall that twenty years ago the only fresh herb in common use was the ubiquitous sprig of parsley that garnished virtually every restaurant dinner plate.

A love of fresh herbs was what drew Noël Richardson and Andrew Yeoman west in 1979. They were Calgarians who had been seduced by the plants they discovered on a visit to British Columbia, and back among the city high-rises, an advertisement in their local newspaper dropped the final piece of the puzzle into place. "For sale," it read, "ten acres of south-sloping hillside overlooking sea and valley. Apple orchard and four-bedroom house."

What Richardson and Yeoman would name Ravenhill Farm had been a working farm since 1910. They purchased the property, then returned to Calgary to wrap up their lives there, spending the inter-vening year reading and fantasizing. Neither had been involved in the culinary arts before, but so what? They considered their new venture just another welcome change of activity, says Yeoman, whose previous careers include geologist, schoolteacher and investment counsellor.

Planning a Herb Garden

First, take a few minutes to imagine your ideal garden. Here are some key questions to consider:

Design: What does your garden look like? Is it formal—kept well trimmed and shaped, like a Victorian garden—or wild, like an English country garden? Perhaps it is a combination.

Function: What herbs are growing in your garden? Start with what you want to use them for: salads? cooking? herbal teas? crafts? medicinal purposes? Have you included any flowers to eat, cut for floral arrangements or preserve?

Theme: Does your garden have a theme? For example, if you love Italian food, you may want to grow everything for pasta sauces: arugula, chives, oregano, basils, garlic and paste tomatoes.

Seating: Do you want to include a place to sit? Gardens are wonderful places to meditate, read, write or enjoy a cup of tea with a friend.

Richardson was formerly a teacher-librarian.

Reading about herbs opened a door into a lost world. Herbs are a scented thread that stitches together ancient Roman cuisine, mediaeval feasts and the Elizabethan era. Yeoman and Richardson's shared passion for cooking, eating, travelling and books soon made them authorities on what their land could produce. Yeoman's forte is vegetables; Richardson is known for her herbs. Collecting seeds, scouring nurseries and talking to fellow enthusiasts soon led to a profusion of varieties to grow in the terraced raised beds. "How many kinds?" is a common question. "Beyond counting!" is the response.

Ravenhill Farm is a tapestry of muted greens: the grey-green of rosemary, the yellow-green of lemon thyme, the subtle hues of sage. Stone walls secure clumps of oregano and a dozen or more kinds of thyme, including rarities such as woolly thyme. Herbs do more than add savour to foods, says Richardson, as she points out a bush of cotton lavender, a grey-coloured, yellow-flowered herb known officially as "santolina" and used in France as a moth deterrent.

But nonedible herbs are rare here. Right from the start, the couple's main interest has been the tasty magic that a handful of insignificant-looking sprigs can work. In the early 1980s, when a distinctive West Coast cuisine was still in its infancy, Yeoman and Richardson started supplying herbs to local chefs. A decade later, they were distributing fresh basil, tarragon, chives and more to over two dozen restaurants. Soon keen amateur chefs were making their way up the winding road to the farm to purchase a pot of rosemary, a packet of dried sage or one of the books Richardson and Yeoman had begun to write—and invariably to pick the brains of the authors. "There's been a huge revolution," says Richardson. "Now more people buy plants than cut herbs. Chefs too."

Running a herb farm is not an easy life; from early March to the end of May, the work is constant. Even in high summer, Richardson and Yeoman put in two hours a day. Viewing themselves as stewards of the land, they nurture it lovingly. Their garden sprawls down a south-facing slope; the soil is thin, and what little organic material there is is leached away by rain. So they add manure from their two breeding ewes and twenty chickens, as well as leaf mould and compost, to the soil.

The soil returns the favour. "We eat out of the vegetable garden all year round," says Yeoman, whose book *A West Coast Kitchen Garden* is a wise and affable introduction to raising not only everyday vegetables but also more exotic varieties such as cardoons and Jerusalem artichokes. Information is just as generously given in person. How do you grow such fat purple eggplants? Easy; give them an early start, protect them with a wood-framed box and plastic sheeting, and raise the sides of the boxes as the plants grow.

The farm's size is enviable, but herbs can flourish even in a small city plot. As a living demonstration, the couple have planted a 54'-square garden, grouping together varieties that demand similar care. One quadrant houses sage, oregano, winter savory and rosemary—sturdy herbs that need little fertilizer or rain. Growing in a box is a flourishing assortment of basils (including the Genovese variety used in authentic pesto), all varieties that need plenty of nourishment and protection from the hot summer sun. Their neighbours are perennial herbs such as fennel and lovage, lovers of rich soil and water. Right next door are annual herbs: dill, coriander, Italian parsley, summer savory and Vietnamese coriander, the last an experiment. Notoriously free-roaming, mint is kept under control in its own bucket.

Yeoman and Richardson both believe in educating others. Penned with a clear eye and a merry heart, *Life at Ravenhill Farm* is Richardson's season-by-season account of the joys of living and cooking with herbs. A visit to Ravenhill Farm is part of the curriculum for local horticultural students. Enthusiasts can join cooking classes in the farm's sunny and spacious kitchen. Richardson is also a popular speaker. Her latest venture is to teach herbal cuisine in conjunction with her youngest daughter, Jenny, a cooking school graduate.

The couple have forged strong links with their local community. In September 1998, they hosted the first Vancouver Island Feast of Fields, a harvest-time celebration of local bounty. Every November, they hold and jury a major crafts fair at Ravenhill. As chair of the local Heritage Commission, Richardson is also involved with designating houses and barns in a region whose first white settler, in 1858, was a Scot named William Thomson. Her role completes a historical circle similar to the seasonal one that governs her life, for it was Thomson's son who built what is now Ravenhill Farm.

Once you have imagined your ideal garden, do a reality check. What kind of space do you have available, in terms of location, size and exposure? How much time are you willing to allocate to your garden: do you have a few minutes each day before going to work or in the evening after supper, or are you a weekend person? If you plan to be away during the summer, do you know someone who can regularly water your plants?

Giving yourself a budget will help you to determine whether you want to buy premixed soil, pots and plants or use what you have available. Gardening doesn't have to cost a lot of money, but supplies can add up quickly unless you are resourceful. Think about whether you want to grow plants in the ground or in containers or both. Basils, chives, marjoram, oregano, parsley, rosemary and scented geraniums grow equally well in a contained space. These herbs can also be grown indoors in winter, but they will need a sunny window or growing lights.

The winter is a wonderful time to research and plan your spring garden. Begin by listing all the plants you would like to grow, and then look up their habits. Measure the space you have to work with and rough out a design on paper. Plot the position of your new beds, plants, paths and accessories, then take your design out to the garden. Mark out areas on the ground and label where you want the plants to go. Now you will be ready to plant when the weather warms and the sun returns. Enjoy!

DARYLE RYO NAGATA'S **HERB-CRUSTED LOIN OF SALT SPRING LAMB WITH OKANAGAN APPLE AND MINT CHUTNEY**

Born and trained in Alberta, Daryle Ryo Nagata has literally cooked his way across Canada (not to mention a stint at noted hotels in London, England). Now executive chef at Vancouver's Waterfront Centre Hotel, he especially enjoys combining Asian flavourings from nearby Chinatown with the freshest British Columbia seafood and produce. His herb garden on the hotel's third-floor terrace provides basil, thyme, Italian flat parsley, sage, chives and lavender for his creations. His culinary philosophy is a classic one: "To eat seasonally, to return to our connection with the land and to practise all the age-old forms of preservation, from drying to pickling."

2 lbs./1 kg lamb loins (boneless, with silver skin removed)
salt and fresh cracked pepper
2 Tbsp./30 mL Dijon mustard
$^1/_2$ cup/125 mL fresh chopped herbs (rosemary, thyme, oregano, chives, parsley or basil)
$^1/_2$ cup/125 mL fresh white bread crumbs

Season lamb loins on both sides with salt and pepper. In a preheated frying pan, sear loins on medium-high heat.

Place lamb on a baking sheet and brush top of each loin lightly with mustard. Combine chopped herbs and bread crumbs and cover tops of brushed loins with mixture.

Bake for 12 minutes at 400°F/200°C for medium-rare. Present with apple and mint chutney. *Serves 6.*

APPLE AND MINT CHUTNEY

1 apple, diced
$^1/_2$ cup/125 mL sugar
6 Tbsp./90 mL cider vinegar
1 Tbsp./15 mL lemon juice
$^1/_2$ tsp./2 mL cumin seed, crushed
$^1/_4$ tsp./1 mL fenugreek seed, crushed
15 leaves fresh mint, cut in julienne strips

Put apple, sugar, vinegar and lemon juice in a heavy-bottom saucepan and cook over medium heat until it reaches a syrupy caramel colour. Add cumin and fenugreek seed. Cook for 5 minutes, cool, and add mint leaves.

Umberto Menghi's **GRILLED CHICKEN BREASTS AND GARLIC-ROSEMARY BUTTER**

MARINADE

5 Tbsp./75 mL white wine
1/4 cup/60 mL brandy
2 Tbsp./30 mL apple cider vinegar
1 tsp./5 mL fresh black pepper, cracked
1 Tbsp./15 mL coarsely chopped garlic
1/4 cup/60 mL olive oil

GARLIC-ROSEMARY BUTTER

6 garlic bulbs, trimmed
1/2 cup/125 mL chopped fresh rosemary
1 1/2 cups/375 mL soft butter
1 Tbsp./15 mL salt
1 tsp./5 mL freshly ground black pepper
juice of 3 lemons

4 chicken breasts
2 Tbsp./30 mL Dijon mustard
1/2 tsp./2 mL salt
3 sprigs fresh sage
3 sprigs fresh thyme
6 sprigs fresh rosemary
2 Tbsp./30 mL olive oil
salt
freshly ground black pepper

For marinade, combine wine, brandy, vinegar and pepper in a saucepan, place over high heat and bring to a boil. Keep mixture boiling until it is reduced by half, then remove from heat and let cool. Add garlic and olive oil. Set aside.

To make garlic-rosemary butter, preheat oven to 350°F/180°C. Place garlic bulbs in a roasting pan and roast until tender and cooked through, about 1 hour. Squeeze out soft pulp from each clove, place in a bowl with rosemary, butter, seasonings and lemon juice, and mix well. Refrigerate for at least 2 hours before using.

Rub chicken breasts with mustard. Place in a baking dish and sprinkle with salt, sage, thyme and 2 sprigs of rosemary. Add marinade to chicken, cover tightly and refrigerate overnight, turning meat several times.

Remove chicken breasts from dish and pat dry. Rub with oil and season with salt and pepper to taste. Place chicken breast, skin side down, on grill and cook over low heat until golden brown and crisp. Baste with garlic-rosemary butter, reserving at least 4 tsp./20 mL. Turn and cook on the other side for 10-12 minutes. Place each chicken breast on a hot dinner plate with 1 tsp./5 mL of garlic rosemary butter on top and garnish with a sprig of rosemary. Serve with baked potatoes or grilled peppers. *Serves 4.*

Andrew Yeoman cuts a bunch of fresh herbs at Ravenhill Farm.

II. Harvesting

The Pacific Northwest is uniquely **blessed** with a plethora of sublime foodstuffs. The region hosts a significant proportion of the world's 20,000 edible species, found in the sea, on the land and in the air. Gatherers—both those who collect for their own use and the wild-crafters who collect for sale—excite our senses with varieties and flavours not found in staid commercial establishments. They increase our range of choice by introducing wonderful new products. Ultimately, they may be instrumental in saving many species of fish, plants and animals. And by putting us more closely in tune with nature, they enrich our lives as well as our diets.

Mushrooms and edible fungi in many colours; berries of every shape and size; and herbs, medicinals, flowers, fish and game are often there just for the taking on the West Coast. But it requires intricate knowledge, experience, time and stamina for harvesters to make their endeavours a success. The best of them are also guided by the ethics of earth care—or stewardship of the land—understanding that taking only what they need will ensure that future generations may also enjoy this natural bounty.

The stories in this chapter feature adventurers, in the best sense of the word: people who, by paying close attention to their immediate environment, open for themselves and for others an awareness of the wonders of abundance and the power of the earth's offerings. Some forage in back alleys and others in remote wilderness areas, but they share the nourishment this region offers so generously. There is much pleasure to be found in opening our eyes to what is around us, and these folks can help to show us the way.

—H.B.

James Barber comes upon a patch of day lilies on one of his foraging missions.

❧ An Urban Forager: James Barber

Whether it's a cluster of purple blackberries or a windfall apple lying by the side of the road, when you come upon food out of the blue, it feels like a gift from nature. City-dwellers believe that the peculiar joy of finding edibles for the taking is a feature of everyday life only in the countryside. Yet in the eyes of at least one experienced forager, the unpaved back laneways winding through Vancouver's residential neighbourhoods are as fruitful as a larder. It is here that chef and cookbook author James Barber likes to hunt and gather.

Today, Barber is known far and wide for his *Urban Peasant* cooking show. But in the early years, when funds were short, he discovered that walking the back lanes of his city provided both a gentle form of entertainment and a frequent source of food. In fact, it was the reality of being able to forage for cooking ingredients within sight of downtown towers that first gave rise to his concept of the urban peasant.

Collecting free food in the city requires an adherence to certain unwritten rules, says Barber, as he reaches up to pick a green apple from a branch that extends overhead. "You exercise common courtesy and common decency. You take one piece of anything, you don't lean over fences—and you don't tell anyone where you got it." Barber may be tightlipped about his sources, but he is openhanded with information. The most productive place for blackberries, he will tell you, is beside railway lines, and the essential tools when you're tracking them down are gloves and a walking stick with a curved handle.

As summer merges into fall, the orange-brown seed heads of roses are plentiful. "Dry the rosehips, bash them up and they make wonderful tea," says Barber. So does clover. Even the most unpromising piece of land can produce yellow chamomile buttons, and an infusion of fresh chamomile "is unbelievably good."

Not all laneway finds are of wild origin. Cultivated plants, however carefully restrained, occasionally make a break for it. Mint may roam underground and pop up far from home. Blown by the breeze, dill seeds from a previous summer can colonize a bare patch of soil. A compost box may produce a trailing, winding zucchini plant, complete with egg-yolk–yellow flowers and finger-sized squash.

Among Barber's favourite finds are chestnut trees, common in Europe, less usual in North America, and differentiated from the more common horse chestnut by their long and pointed leaves. Wear gloves when you're on the hunt for chestnuts, advises Barber—"They have lots of prickles." If you want hazelnuts, he says, "Look for catkins in the spring and remember where the trees are. *Picking* the nuts is not the way to do it. You have to shake the tree."

Barber also knows where to find walnut trees, including the black walnut variety whose shells are so hard, he says, "that you pretty well need a bench vise to break them." Years of ambling along urban byways have also taught him the hiding places of unusual fruits such as mulberries and quince, a variety that looks like a fuzzy misshapen apple.

To be harvested and stored up too are the treats for the eye that occur unexpectedly as you stroll along these peaceful paths. Barber points out a maple tree, still green in early September. Wait a month, he says, and it will explode into a fireball of glowing reds, oranges and golds: "And maple leaves are for making dinner tables look wonderful." Nearby, black and claret-coloured laurel berries shine in the autumn sun. They are nonedible, but, as Barber points out, the visual feast of foraging can be as nourishing to the spirit as foraged foods are to the body.

In the middle of a sentence, he suddenly pauses, hooks his foraging stick around a ground-level bramble and pulls it aside to reveal a cluster of fungi. "You have to *look* all the time," he stresses. "The trick with foraging is to teach yourself to see."

JAMES BARBER'S **FISH WITH HAZELNUT CRUST**

"Fish with a bread-crumb crust can get soggy very easily, and fish in batter can get soggy and greasy. But a nut crust doesn't absorb the oil, and it stays crisp and crunchy. It also develops a nice nutty (what else?) flavour and turns the plainest piece of fish into a special occasion. I put nut crusts on salmon fillets, cod and halibut, and they always produce enthusiastic smiles around the table," says Barber.

Nuts are easy to buy, and they always improve with 15 minutes of roasting on a cookie sheet in a 250°F/120°C oven. The best thing you can do is to gather or buy nuts in the fall, when they're at their freshest. Simply freeze them in plastic bags and take out a handful whenever you need them.

2 Tbsp./30 mL oil
2 fillets white fish or salmon
1 egg, beaten (just the whites if you prefer)
1 lemon, zest and juice
¹/₂ cup/125 mL hazelnuts (or any other kind of nut), finely chopped
2 Tbsp./30 mL parsley, chopped

Heat oil in a fry pan over medium heat. Dredge fish in beaten egg and sprinkle with chopped hazelnuts. Add fish to fry pan and cook for 3 minutes on each side, until nuts are nice and toasted. Serve with a squeeze of lemon and some parsley and lemon zest sprinkled over top. *Serves 2.*

❦ Painting with a Regional Palette: Sinclair Philip

Edible landscaping at its finest surrounds Sinclair Philip outside Sooke Harbour House.

Some chefs view the world as their larder, combining mahi mahi or Dover sole jetted in from half a world away with lemongrass from Thailand, rice from Japan and out-of-season vegetables from warmer climates. Others—an increasing number—recognize that the cornerstone of the best cuisine is local ingredients gathered in season; and no one in B.C. has done more to promote this trend than culinary pioneer Sinclair Philip, owner of Vancouver Island's Sooke Harbour House. Set on a scenic bay less than an hour's drive from Victoria, his white clapboard inn has recently been expanded—for the second time—to house the growing number of gourmets who come to sample what is described as the most authentic regional cuisine in North America.

Philip makes no concessions: he uses only foods gathered, picked or raised within the smallest radius possible, refracting them through his unique culinary prism. The cuisine that results is truly one of a kind, as a typical dinner menu reveals. Sooke sturgeon is napped in a raspberry and sweet cicely sauce and served with glazed beets and maple-roasted celeriac. Cider-marinated East Sooke lamb shoulder comes with a spiced McIntosh apple and marjoram sauce. Twin terrines—one of smoked salmon and goat cheese, the other of coho salmon and asparagus—are accompanied by a pear and balsamic vinaigrette and trout roe. Octopus may be served with blueberry dressing, wild spring salmon with rosehip-mustard sauce. At Sooke Harbour House, it is normal for a salad to contain more than two dozen different leaves and flowers, and even a simple white wine spritzer may be garnished with clove pinks and hauntingly flavoured with an infusion of grand fir needles, lavender, lemon verbena, lemon thyme and fennel.

Canadian-born, with a doctorate in political economics from Grenoble University, Sinclair Philip has been intrigued by seafood

since he was a boy, when he made all his pocket money by selling crabs he caught off the Dundarave pier in West Vancouver. In the years that followed his interest led to the creation of numerous seafood recipes. Friends who sampled them were enthusiastic, and Philip and his wife, Fredrica, also an economist, moved to Canada from abroad in 1978 with the intention of opening a restaurant.

Sooke Harbour House, in operation since 1928, was up for sale. It was ideal: fish and seafood would be available right on Philip's doorstep, and a year later the inn was again open for business. Its rooms were decorated with antiques, art and crafts; flowers, homemade cookies and a decanter of port awaited each guest.

But the comfort, and even the view of ocean and mountains, were nothing compared to what diners found on their plates, and soon the exceptional food and its provenance were receiving accolades internationally. Sooke Harbour House has been featured in French and German food magazines and profiled extensively in the North American media. Consistently rated among the top ten restaurants in the country, it was named top restaurant in the world for authentic local cuisine in a 1997 *Gourmet* magazine poll. One restaurant critic referred to it as "the Mother House of Canadian cuisine." Philip himself has been described as "a walking encyclopedia of food knowledge." Chefs vie to work at Sooke Harbour House, and some of the country's most innovative young talent has graduated from its kitchen.

Philip's years of living in France taught him that having only a local seasonal pantry to draw from forces cooks to develop new and interesting ways of working with familiar ingredients. The same can happen in Canada, he believes: "We have the raw materials in this country to do something quite incredible."

He is upset by the slow degradation of what we put on our tables. "People haven't eaten a real chicken in forty years," he laments, as he describes the contamination present in today's foods. At Sooke Harbour House, organic produce, lamb, rabbit, pheasant, Muscovy duck, and free-range chickens and eggs come from neighbouring farms. Instead of olive oil, chefs use locally made nut oils. The only items not produced locally are coffee, orange juice and chocolate, on the menu simply because of guest demand.

The restaurant is justifiably famous for the glorious variety of seafood that graces its tables. Fresh limpets and purple shore crabs are among the local gleanings that show up in dishes from Philip's kitchen. He dives when he can with a commercial diver to see what the ocean will yield and trades information with local fishers and shellfish harvesters about the ebb and flow of marine populations. Razor clams are becoming hard to find, he says; butter clams too. "Abalone are shrinking in number, and I don't know why. Octopus are proliferating."

Few of the many fish varieties that swim in local waters show up in local markets, Philip points out. Names? He can give you dozens, among them skate, horse mackerel, wolf fish, cabezon, sculpin, idiot rockfish, red Irish lord and pelagic sturgeon, and flying squid, with its tender and sweet mantle meat. "The reason we don't use these fish is largely ignorance," he says. "Some of them are exported to the Far East, where they are considered to be very good. Other kinds are discarded by both sport and commercial fishermen without any valid reason."

The two acres of land under cultivation at Sooke Harbour House, their soil fed a rich diet of compost and seaweed, grow a cornucopia of herbs and flowers, all of which Philip uses in one way or another. Calendula petals flavour buckwheat bread sticks. Winter savory and garden sage are kneaded into a rye flour and buttermilk loaf. Tuberous begonia petals or johnny-jump-ups lend their essences to butters. Philip estimates that he works with as many as five hundred different flowers, herbs, salad greens and vegetables in the course of a year, some grown in his garden, some the result of foraging trips. As he walks through the grounds, he identifies some of the many species: passion fruit vines; tiny red and white strawberries; houttuynia, a Japanese herb with red-edged leaves; tiny, flat velvet mint; nodding onion; Indian celery; and a Chinese artichoke whose root grows in a spiral shape. It's a botanical text come to life.

Fish, flower or herb, "we find what's there and then make up the menu," says Philip. "Often at 4:00 P.M. we still don't know what we'll be serving for dinner that night."

SINCLAIR PHILIP'S **WILD WEST COAST MUSSEL SOUP WITH STINGING NETTLE CREAM**

$^1/_2$ lb./250 g wild stinging nettles
2 cups/500 mL whipping cream, divided into 2 portions
24 wild or cultivated mussels
2 cups/500 mL fish stock or water
1 Tbsp./15 mL peeled ginger, minced
2 Tbsp./30 mL sunflower oil
2 medium shallots, peeled and chopped
$^1/_2$ cup/125 mL dry white wine
1 Tbsp./15 mL garlic, minced
$^1/_2$ cup/125 mL sorrel (wild or French), chopped

In a large saucepan, bring four cups of water to a boil. Wearing rubber gloves, wash nettles, removing stems and damaged leaves. Add to boiling water, cover and cook over high heat 2 minutes or until wilted and bright green. Strain, shaking out excess water. Place in a blender, add 1 cup cream and process until smooth. Pass through a medium strainer and keep warm.

Scrub mussels, removing any fibrous strings (beards). Discard any mussels that are open. Heat a large saucepan over high heat and add stock or water and bring to a boil. Add ginger and mussels. Reduce heat to medium, cover and steam 3-4 minutes, or until all mussels are open. (After 4-5 minutes, discard any that have not opened).

Shell mussels and transfer to a separate bowl, reserving 4 mussels in the shell for garnish. Pour liquid through strainer to remove any bits of sand or shell. Set aside and keep warm.

Heat a saucepan over medium heat for 1 minute. Add oil and shallots. Cook, stirring, until shallots are translucent. Add wine and continue to cook until liquid is reduced by two-thirds. Add garlic, remaining cream, strained cooking liquor and half the mussels. Pour into a blender and process until smooth.

Return soup to saucepan. Add remaining mussels. Heat over medium heat until simmering, and stir in 2 Tbsp./30 mL of sorrel. Ladle into heated soup bowls. Garnish each with a spoonful of nettle cream, top with reserved mussels in shells, and sprinkle with remaining sorrel. *Serves 4.*

❦ Harvesting Nature's Bounty: Nancy Turner

Like all aboriginal peoples, those who lived on the West Coast once depended entirely on nature for their survival. As sources of food, materials and medicines, wild plants were especially valuable. Accordingly, says Nancy Turner, these plants were central to First Nations lore, ceremonies and traditional knowledge.

A professor of environmental studies at the University of Victoria, Turner is a leading authority on ethnobotany, the link between people and plants. It's a passion that dates back to her childhood—in elementary school, she remembers, she fed a salad of dandelion leaves to some of her friends. By the late 1960s, Turner had become especially intrigued by the ways in which B.C.'s First Nations used plants. Which ones did people eat? How did they cook with them? Regular sessions with elder Christopher Paul of the Tsartlip community on B.C.'s Saanich Peninsula provided a wealth of answers.

As Turner continued her research, travelling along the coast and throughout the southern interior, she became increasingly aware of the significance of what she was learning. "Most of the elders have now passed away," she says twenty years later. "It was essential to write their knowledge down. The residential school system, in which the government removed aboriginal children from their homes, resulted in a general loss of knowledge of plants and their uses. And a lot of elders were very concerned that even if succeeding generations had the information they would not always be able to find and identify the plants, because habitats were becoming more fragile."

In 1979, Turner and coauthor Adam Szczawinski, then curator of botany at the Royal British Columbia Museum, published *Edible Wild Fruits and Nuts of Canada*. The book rekindled an interest in the natural bounty of the land, reminding people about the pleasures of foraging in the late summer sun and bringing home baskets brimming with delicious berries. It reminded them too that this abundance could be preserved, made into jams, jellies or wine for the colder months.

Eating seasonally is something aboriginal peoples have always known about. In many cultures, roots and new sprouts nourished people in the spring. Summer was a time for fruits and berries. Fall reaped a harvest of nuts, bulbs and roots, and stored foods fed people throughout the winter. Pacific crab apples, for instance, the only

apples native to British Columbia, were picked in late summer and early fall, then kept underwater in cedar boxes where they grew sweeter as the winter wore on. Many other foods were carefully dried.

The meadows, forests, freshwater marshes, swamps and tidal wetlands of British Columbia once nurtured equally varied vegetation. By trading foods—fish from the coast for root vegetables from the interior, camas bulbs for blueberries—people traditionally added new items to their daily diets. Many plants were multipurpose. Skunk cabbage roots had a medicinal use, and the plant's leaves became "Indian wax paper" to line baskets and drying racks. The inner stem of fireweed was eaten raw by several groups; others used the long leaves in a tea.

The bulb of the blue camas, a member of the lily family, was cooked slowly in an underground pit to make it digestible, palatable and of maximal nutritional value. The long, slim rhizomes of springbank clover (early settlers called it "Indian spaghetti") were also a staple. The roots of Pacific silverweed, a yellow-flowered relative of the strawberry, were dug, tied in bundles, pit-cooked and eaten. Not all edible underground plants were what we commonly think of as root vegetables. As its name suggests, rice root, another member of the lily family, looks exactly like a ball of rice grains.

Although Turner started by recording just the names and uses of plants, increasingly her interests in environmental issues and ethnobotany converged. As she notes, some plants have disappeared, and others are not as prolific as they were. "At one time," she says, "you wouldn't take wild potatoes unless they were as large as a golf ball. Now you're lucky to find them the size of marbles."

To her initial surprise, Turner discovered during her research that First Nations peoples amassed enough knowledge about the land they relied on for sustenance to develop a form of cultivation. Berry bushes were "pruned"; once huckleberries or salmonberries had been picked, the older branches would be snapped off to increase productivity the following year. Saskatoon berry bushes were cut back for the same reason. Salal berries were plucked by the branch in intact clusters. Sometimes people even transplanted wild berry bushes and other plants.

Three decades of working in her chosen field have provided Turner with "many hours of sheer bliss and fascination." On one occasion, she camped on the coast with an aboriginal friend who had not been back to his home for forty years. "He knew exactly what we'd see at a certain bend in the river," says Turner. Another time, while working with Nuxalk elders from Bella Coola, she remembers "going out and getting the inner bark of cottonwood, which was once an important food. There's a certain time of year when it's just right, when the sap is coming up, and you can scrape off the gelatinous layer between the bark and the tree." Finding this with the elders was, Turner recalls, a moving experience. "They hadn't tasted it since they were children."

Aboriginal Cultivation Practices

Did aboriginal peoples, long described as hunter-fisher-gatherers, actually cultivate plants, developing and changing "natural" plant communities through their actions? Yes, according to Kwakwaka'wakw historian Daisy Sewid-Smith (Mayanilth) and Kwakwaka'wakw hereditary chief and elder Adam Dick (Kwaxistala). When asked if the "grandfather" part of the rice root was removed simply to clean off the root, or rather because it might grow into another plant, Adam Dick was adamant: "That's what it does. That's why it was replanted."

Nancy Turner: I see. So it's just like gardening, really.

Adam Dick: It is gardening!

Daisy Sewid-Smith: People didn't believe that we did this. They think that nature just grows on its own. But our people felt to get more harvest, and bigger berries, they did the same things a farmer does.

T'akilakw (Manufactured ground)

Adam Dick: It was all important: *texwsus* (springbank clover), *tliksam* (silverweed), *q'weniy'* (Nootka lupine) and *xukwem* (rice root). Every family had pegs and owned their little plots in the flats. They would dig the soft ground . . . so it will grow better every year. Well, I guess, fertilizing, cultivating, that's the word for it.

They had a stick called *k'ellákw*. It was yew wood, three-cornered, like a three-cornered file . . . when they're breaking the earth. They have a knob on the end that you hang onto. They're all different sizes. It was really sharp, like a pencil. I used to dig with that. It's hard. 'Cause when you push it down and you put all your weight on it when you're breaking, softening that ground . . . I guess that *texwsus* and all the other roots grow better when it's softened up.

Replanting

Propagules are called *GaGemp* (Grandfather). Adam Dick recalled that when he was a boy of nine or ten, "That was my job to pick off the bottom of that 'golf ball' called the *GaGemp*. They told me to pull them off and throw them back in the [plot] . . . It's brown, it's awfully soft. Well, it's a root, eh?"

Weeding

Adam Dick described weeding practices:

"We *sixa* it, we call it 'sixa' when you pull all the weeds out of there and just what you want is left, like the *texwsus* and *tliksam* and the *q'weniy'*. If there's lots of weeds, it doesn't grow that good, that's why they *t'akilakw*, they look after it . . . See, they looked after it, different families."

Pruning

A range of berries were also "pruned" to enhance productivity. Daisy Sewid-Smith and Chief Adam Dick recalled that red huckleberries, salmonberries and stink currants were routinely pruned after the annual harvest by breaking the branches off.

"As soon as we clean the tree out [i.e., pick all the berries], we *tl'eXw7id*, we break them so the berries would grow plentifully later. A lot of people think we never touched the wild berries. But we did. We cultivated them. We pruned them. Especially *gwadems* (red huckleberries). When they finished picking the *gwadems*, they break the tops off. *Qw'alhem* (salmonberries) too. My grandma told me that if you let it grow this high [two yards or so], it doesn't produce much berries . . . She says the water, it's hard going up there, I guess, when it's too tall."

Transplanting

Adam Dick described how, as a young man, he had transplanted high-bush cranberry from the edge of the bog meadow at Kingcome Inlet to the area behind his house:

"I tried planting them behind our house, in Kingcome. And the late wife, we had lots. But she used to pick them and jar them. I transplanted them from up the river, from the edge of the meadows, that's where you find them. When I'm trapping up the river there when I was quite young and that turned to *k'wemdekw* [ripe and soft] right on in the fall, so I thought, you know, pull them out and they're really easy to grow. They multiplied behind the house, and my mother used to go there and pick."

Ownership

When asked about Kwakwaka'wakw ownership of the bog cranberry beds at Kingcome, Adam Dick said that they were so extensive anyone could go there to pick. He and Daisy Sewid-Smith elaborated further on "ownership" of resources:

"Everybody had their own berry patches, just like everybody had their own clam beds. Things like [salal patches]. Yeah, salmonberries and all that, all kinds of berries, wild crab apple, you just don't go [out and pick]. There's certain places that a certain family goes, especially that wild crab apples. Our family used to go over here. And the other families go over here.

"They got markers too, for *celXw*. Oh, yes, they have pegs, you put pegs all around the tree. Especially the wild crab apples. You just pick up those little sticks and you just peg, put it around the [tree]. Any kind of sticks. If you can get cedar, that would be good. Anything that's pegged, you know it's someone's."

DOLLY WATTS'S YEL'ISS (WHIPPED SOAPBERRIES)

As the daughter and granddaughter of clan chiefs, Dolly Watts grew up learning to make and serve food for traditional feasts. In 1990 she began selling her favourite bread—"Grandma's Bannock"—at the University of British Columbia, where she was studying anthropology. That led to a catering business and eventually to Liliget Feast House, a Vancouver restaurant that specializes in Northwest Coast First Nations food.

Iss (soapberries) thrive among jack pine trees and in shady areas. For a very short period, about two weeks, the velvety, dark-green bushes have green, shiny, oblong berries. The berries turn a warm salmon pink and finally red, which means they are ripe. They are picked at each stage. When ripe, a sturdy plastic bag is placed under the bushes and the branches are hit gently with a stick. Traditionally a cedar woven mat (*ha'nii yetsis*, meaning "on which to hit soapberries") was used in the same manner.

If the berries are picked green, whipping them produces a white "mousse." Salmon-coloured berries produce a soft pink "mousse," ripe berries a darker-pink one. As berries ripen, their taste becomes more distinct. Before the egg beater arrived to the Gitwangak people, mousse was made by squeezing berries with very clean, oil-free hands, then adding water and beating them in a circular motion. If the mousse is watery, more berries are added.

Mousse is ready to eat when it resembles stiffly beaten egg whites. It has to be eaten right away; otherwise, it softens and must be whipped again.

❦ The Return of the Salmon: Ben Davidson

A quick flash of silver that can arc like a shooting star. A fish with the uncanny ability to return to the waters that gave it birth. Mysterious and magnificent, the salmon has always had a central place in the lives and cosmologies of many First Nations groups. The rivers of British Columbia once boiled with these mighty fish. For the Haida people in their island home of Haida Gwaii (the Queen Charlotte Islands), salmon remain an important source of food. While the fish have dropped in number, old ways of catching and preserving them live on.

First Nations carver Ben Davidson turns his skills to pumpkins.

Artist Ben Davidson doesn't remember how old he was the first time he went to the Yakoun River to see the sockeye salmon running. "We had a fish camp there," Ben recalls, "a little A-frame house right on the river where we'd stay for three or four days."

Ben's mother, Susan Davidson, spent extended periods of time on Haida Gwaii, and the spring salmon catch remains vivid in her memory. "We would go to a place about thirty miles from the village at the mouth of the Yakoun River, where it's tidal. They would put gill nets across the river." The windows of the small cabins lit by oil lanterns would glow amber in the black northern night. "I remember it as a magical time," says Susan. "There was co-operation and competition. A sense of going back in time. When the salmon came, you worked with nature."

Working with nature meant setting your net at slack water, maybe at 3:00 A.M., and then taking good care of it; tidal debris blocking the mesh could make the nets visible to the salmon. "You were working the nets all the time," says Susan, "going back and forth in little dinghies, picking out twigs and branches. And everybody had this sense that you weren't trying to catch every fish that went up the river."

"There'd be uncles and aunts there, and my great-grandmother," recalls Ben Davidson. "When the fish hit, it was lots of fun. Five or ten might hit all at once. That was chaos." It was also a lot of hard work. No refrigeration meant that all the salmon had to be cleaned and prepared right away.

Some of the fish was eaten on the spot. "We'd have a barbecue at the river, fifteen or twenty people, all the elders," says Ben. In the traditional Haida way of cooking salmon, the whole fish is impaled on a red cedar stake about four feet long; smaller cedar stakes are woven through the fish to keep it in place as it cooks over an open fire, first on one side, then the other. When ready, it is served with dried seaweed, oolichan grease and herring roe.

By the time Davidson was a boy, much of the catch was canned. Families came equipped, many with big pressure cookers—those without used a large oil drum instead—and a machine called a "sealer," which attaches lids to metal cans. Once gutted, the salmon was cut into chunks that would fit a pint or half-pint jar. Notches in a cedar plank cutting board indicated where the fish should be sliced. "You could see how many times it had been cut in the same spot," Ben says. "We canned at the end of spring, end of May, early June. You'd use the fish till the next spring. You gave a lot of it away, to people who couldn't get out to fish or to friends who dropped by to visit." Sometimes, before being canned, the fish was soaked in a brine of water, salt and brown sugar, then smoked over green alder branches.

Some fish were smoked for a day in the on-site smokehouse. One method was to cut them first into strips called "kippers" that were shaped like a pair of pants so they could be hung easily over the cedar drying racks. In another method, fish were slit open and then each side cut open again so that the smoke could penetrate more easily. Called "newspapers," these could be folded and stacked to last all winter.

Being there for the salmon run was part of Ben Davidson's life and an important part of his learning. Today an apprentice with his father, noted artist Robert Davidson, he still spends four or five months each year in his ancestral home. It's a time to go out on the beach, to enjoy the wilderness with no one else around, to recall the excitement of seeing the silvery fish of ancient lore return to their birthplace.

Making Indian Candy (Dried Salmon Strips)

Dolly Watts

I am Gitksan first and Nuu-chah-nulth by marriage. My first seven years were spent at my birthplace, Gitwangak (Kitwanga), and I lived there sporadically thereafter. At seven years old, I was in a hospital, and then the next ten years in the Port Alberni Indian residential school. I married a Tseshaht from Port Alberni whose grandfather was a Maliliqulan chief on Village Island. I lived there for the next thirty years.

Food was a preoccupation for both nations, first for survival and secondly for celebrations. Food dripped with oil, and pungent aromas quickly filled the home or the feast house.

During five months of each year, June to October, berries, vegetables, salmon and venison were gathered and preserved. Berries from the forest were picked in great quantity. In early spring, children ran into the bushes to pick "saski," or salmonberry shoots. In Gitwangak, we "scaped" or scraped pine sap when it began to harden. Later, when the sap hardened, we broke pieces off these "pine noodles" and chewed them like gum.

There was variety in our diet, and yet the main food item was salmon.

Ghy'hooks (Gitwangak) or *Ups-qwee* (Tsesaht)

To make *ups-qwee*, fresh salmon is filleted in uniform thickness, about 1/4". The strips are then placed over a pole overnight, after which they are turned over and left to dry some more. The semi-dried salmon is then skewered and left to dry completely for a further four days. The strips are stored in a cool, dry place—best in a wooden box that allows some air to circulate—or else bagged and frozen. These salmon strips usually last about one year without refrigeration.

The Gitksan keep the fillets, the *ghy'hooks*, attached to the whole salmon. When the whole salmon is dried, there are four folds. This occurs because fillets are sliced starting from the centre of the salmon and working towards the outside, stopping about 1/4" from the edge. The fillet is flipped over. The right side of the salmon has two thin fillets, one strip containing the spine. The whole salmon is placed over a pole, skin side down. The drying process takes a few days, during which time the salmon is turned daily. When dry, it is skewered and moved up high, where it continues to receive some smoke. The *ghy'hooks* are detached only when the salmon is going to be "burned" or roasted over an open fire. Today, the dried salmon is roasted in the oven.

To eat *ghy'hooks* or *ups-qwee*, break off a piece and eat as is or salt slightly and dip in butter or oolichan oil. You can also soak overnight and then heat by covering the strips with boiling water. Serve with boiled potatoes or rice, onions and vegetables.

Left:
Even in the city, herbs flourish easily, providing tasty raw material for salads, seasonings and, in this case, tea.

Below left:
You're never too young to savour fresh-picked corn at a corn roast. Here Kaz Takahashi (right) introduces Cade McMeekin to a summertime ritual at Fraser Common Farm.

Below right:
Organic grapes ripen and swell in the hot Okanagan sun.

Above left:

Harvested in Tofino, on the west coast of Vancouver Island, crabs and gooseneck barnacles fuel inventive local cuisine.

Above:

"Urban Peasant" James Barber (second from right) hooks an audience at Granville Market after Dark.

Left:

Nature always provides, however remote the location.

DOLLY WATTS'S **FISH HASH**

"I came from a family of fourteen," says Dolly Watts, *"and this recipe stretched our budget. Mom used leftover baked, boiled or smoked salmon. Sometimes she boiled the backbones and scraped all of the salmon off those. Canned salmon can be used too."*

12 nugget potatoes, peeled and thinly sliced
1 medium onion, sliced
1 lb./500 g cooked salmon, flaked (or two 14 oz./425 g tins)
2 tsp./10 mL canola oil
salt and white pepper to taste

Over medium heat, fry onions and potatoes until light brown, about 4-5 minutes. Add salmon and heat through. Season with salt and pepper, and serve warm with vegetables and your favourite condiment or sauce. *Serves 4.*

The Joy of Mushrooms: Bill Jones

A mushroom is one of nature's mysteries. Flourishing in dank, dimly lit surroundings, it appears overnight as if from nowhere. Unnervingly cool to the touch, it has a fleshy, almost alien texture. Colours range from the orange and sulphurous yellow of the variety called "chicken of the woods" to the creamy white of the oyster mushroom. A mushroom can be the size of a thumbnail or grow to weigh several pounds. Some are so toxic that even a small taste may be fatal, others so delectable that prestigious restaurants pay high prices for them.

Bill Jones discovers every mushroom picker's dream—a patch of chanterelles.

Canadian chef and cookbook writer Bill Jones was living in England when he first discovered the pleasures of mushroom hunting. "There was a bounty of horse mushrooms on the South Downs," he remembers, and searching for these "little pieces of treasure" quickly became addictive. A culinary apprenticeship in the Alsace took Jones to a region of France renowned for cèpes (otherwise known as porcini). "I got into those and what was called a quiche mushroom there but is known as a parasol mushroom here. Both were amazingly tasty. I found I could supplement my income by hiking and foraging in the afternoon. Sometimes I was getting 20 pounds in three hours." Back in Canada, working as a chef, Jones hooked up with local mushroom brokers. He also joined the Vancouver Mycological Society. "Then it was a matter of going out with experts and slowly building up my confidence."

British Columbia is a good place to hunt for mushrooms, says Jones. On a walk in the Cowichan Valley, he once found twenty different varieties in a two-hour period: angel wings; chanterelles; ribbon-shaped, highly aromatic cauliflower fungus; thin-stalked fairy ring mushrooms; fluorescent-orange lobster mushrooms; and flavourful hedgehog mushrooms.

Despite their often romantic names, the process of foraging for mushrooms is far from idyllic. In the Pacific Northwest, wild fungi can be picked from the middle of August up until Hallowe'en; the end of the season is determined by the first heavy frost. For much of that time the air is damp and chilly, and the mist almost heavy enough to qualify as rain. Many prized varieties of mushrooms hide deep in the dense woods of steep mountainsides.

The picker's first challenge is spotting the mushrooms. As your eyes grow used to the filtered light, Jones writes in the Mycological Society's *Mushroom Cookbook*, "what was initially a chaotic collage of dark greens and browns gradually becomes subtle shades of tawny, chocolate, green, rusty red and occasional flashes of white. Experienced mushroom foragers tune themselves in to their environment. You look for subtle variations in familiar patterns, protruding colours, disturbed mats of leaves, anything that catches the darting search of your eyes."

One of a mushroom picker's favourite sights is the flash of yellow-orange that signals a chanterelle. Also prized by gourmets is the boletus, with its huge swollen stem and spongy underside that begins as white-beige in colour and then takes on greenish and yellowish hues. Edible too—and easy for beginners to spot and identify—are angel wing mushrooms that grow on fallen leaf-bearing logs. There's also the variety Jones calls "SBMS"—"small, brown mushrooms"—some with hallucinogenic properties and many of little interest. "There are about two thousand varieties of mushrooms in the region, but only fifty are culinarily desirable. Many are edible but bland or unpleasant in flavour. Just because you can eat a mushroom doesn't necessarily mean you want to."

Nor do you pick every mushroom you find. "A good fungi-phile will respect the environment around the mushroom," Jones says.

The Survivors' Banquet

Many amateur mushroom hunters and keen gourmets in B.C.'s Lower Mainland eventually find their way to the Vancouver Mycological Society, a not-for-profit organization whose driving force is to introduce the public to the marvellous world of mushrooms. Experts lead enthusiasts on guided hikes. A newsletter reports on global events. An annual display at Vancouver's VanDusen Botanical Garden gives beginners the chance to learn about various species. And each January, when they have reluctantly ceased mushroom hunting for another year, members of the society host a potluck Survivors' Banquet. Admission is $2, most tote a bottle of wine, and everyone brings a dish that contains, or in some way alludes to, mushrooms.

The fare is inventive and delicious. A Persian dish of apples stuffed with lentils, rice and winter chanterelles, seasoned with tamarind and cumin, sits alongside a platter of plump bratwurst on a bed of Portobello mushrooms. Sometimes handwritten labels reveal ingredients: a thick soup contains chanterelles and smoked russula mushrooms; little pockets of bean curd are stuffed with rice and shiitakes. There are mushrooms in muffins and muffins that *look* like mushrooms and mushrooms imparting their earthy fragrance to noodle and pasta dishes. With extraordinary accuracy, one participant has even shaped and hand-painted cookie dough into a semblance of woodland fungi.

The event is a nostalgic reminder of safaris past—and a tantalizing taste of those to come. "You're all looking for the same thing," one mycophile explains, "but you have to keep the location secret. You're going up hill and down dale, and suddenly the sun catches the gleam of those angel wings. It's like being an old-time prospector and suddenly finding a seam of gold."

Some he breaks into pieces and scatters to distribute the spores for next year's harvest. He may have learned from his first foraging partner that "humans are merely an advanced form of the truffle-hunting pigs," but in Jones's opinion that's no reason to be hoggish when you're out looking for mushrooms.

BILL JONES'S **MUSHROOM CHOWDER**

This recipe calls for chanterelles, but any type of edible wild or cultivated mushroom will also work in this versatile soup; try Portobello, crimini, shiitake or boletus.

2 Tbsp./30 mL butter or olive oil
1 lb./500 g chanterelle mushrooms (*Cantharellus cibarius*), sliced
¹/₂ lb./250 g cauliflower fungus (*Sparassis crispa*)
1 Tbsp./15 mL garlic, minced
2 large onions, diced
4 Tbsp./60 mL flour
1 qt./1 L chicken (or vegetable) stock
1 qt./1 L milk
2 large potatoes, peeled and diced
2 Tbsp./30 mL minced fresh herbs (rosemary, marjoram, parsley, lovage)
salt and pepper to taste

In a large pot, heat oil over medium-high heat for 30 seconds. Add garlic, onions and mushrooms and sauté for 5 minutes, or until mushrooms begin to soften. Sprinkle flour over top, stir well and sauté 1-2 minutes.

Add chicken stock, milk and potatoes. Stir often while bringing to a boil, then reduce heat and simmer for 15 minutes or until potatoes are tender. Add herbs and season with salt and pepper. Serve piping hot with sourdough bread. *Serves 4.*

CAROL CHOW'S **ROASTED BREAST OF FREE-RANGE CHICKEN WITH CHANTERELLE MUSHROOMS AND HERB JUS**

"It's so much fun to work with what we have in British Columbia," says Carol Chow, chef at West Vancouver's Beach Side Café. Trained at the Dubrulle French Culinary School, Chow spent five and a half years in the kitchen at Bishop's before moving to her current location in 1992. She is famous for uncomplicated but highly flavourful dishes.

4–8 free-range chicken breasts
1 Tbsp./15 mL olive oil
1 Tbsp./15 mL Dijon mustard
1 Tbsp./15 mL fresh herbs (rosemary, oregano, thyme or savory)
salt and pepper to taste
1/2 lb./250 g fresh chanterelle mushrooms, preferably small ones
1 Tbsp./15 mL garlic, sliced thin
1 cup/250 mL chicken stock
2 Tbsp./30 mL unsalted butter

Preheat oven to 400°F/200°C. Heat oil in oven-proof pan. Season chicken with Dijon, herbs, salt and freshly ground pepper. Place skin side down in hot pan and sear until golden brown. Turn chicken over and place in oven for 12 minutes, or until juices run clear.

Remove chicken from pan and set aside. Add mushrooms and garlic to pan and sauté for 2 minutes. Add stock and cook until reduced by one-half. Remove from heat and add butter.

Assemble mushrooms on hot plates. Slice chicken on bias and place over mushrooms. Serve with fresh asparagus and new potatoes. *Serves 4.*

❦ Dinner on the Doorstep: Rod Butters

Every morning, Rod Butters tunes in to a Vancouver radio station, listens to news of urban traffic gridlocked here and bottle-necked there, and smiles. Then he walks out the door for the thirty-second commute from his home in the woods to the kitchen of the Wickaninnish Inn, perched on the wild west coast of Vancouver Island.

Butters has come full circle on a culinary journey that started amid the city towers of Toronto and eventually brought him back to his native province with his beliefs intact. Food trends come and go, but Butters has consistently cooked regional cuisine—whose secret, he believes, is simply a matter of tracking down the best possible local ingre-dients and treating them with respect and imagination.

Brought in a year before the Wickanninish Inn opened in August 1996, Butters not only planned the kitchen at the Pointe but also had a hand in the restaurant design, right down to the plates on the table. "Look," he points out, "no rim. The emphasis is on the food." He's proud of being a work-ing chef; he and his staff make everything daily from scratch, including half a dozen different kinds of bread, three kinds of ice cream, and sorbets that often feature the salal berries he harvests on Chesterman Beach.

Seafood is caught within hailing distance. "These came right off the rocks," says Butters, holding out a crate of knobbly, almost primeval-looking creatures. They are local gooseneck barnacles,

Within sight of the Wickanninish Inn, chef Rod Butters finds a popu-lar delicacy, gooseneck barnacles.

revered in Spain but unknown to most North Americans. "I've got some nice octopus that I'm going to do something with too," he says, lifting the lid off a plastic container to reveal a pink and grey ten-pounder curled inside.

In Tofino, the nearest town, Butters buys sweetly succulent Indian candy. The restaurant's oysters come from Oyster Jim, who cultivates bivalves for roasting with extra-hard shells that keep the meat inside meltingly tender. "And you can't get any better crab than the crab here," says Butters. "We grab them out of our own crab pot at the town dock."

Neighbouring forests are scoured for mushrooms. Local farmers supply free-range eggs. A nearby veterinarian makes goat cheese; Butters buys most of the thirty pounds she produces each week. Wild blue-berries, blackberries and salal berries are made into desserts and into preserves and chutneys for the winter months, when the menu's emphasis shifts towards local lamb and game.

Because of the region's dense forest, little produce is grown in the immediate area. But by the time of the inn's first anniversary, Butters had found an organic farm on the east coast of the island. "Greens like you've never had before," he rejoices, as well as potatoes, tomatoes, beets and apples.

Recently, Butters planted a garden in a meadow just beyond the carved cedar porte-cochère of the inn. Before he selected the seeds for it, he monitored the weather for an entire year, noting where the sun fell and how the wind and salt air affected the land where he planned to grow herbs and vegetables.

These days, Butters also serves a new find from the sea. "Hold both of your hands together and they're that size," he says, to convey the massiveness of the acorn barnacles that local harvesters have recently begun to bring him. It's the meat that intrigues him. "It's only the size of a finger, but intense and crablike." That's B.C. cuisine, he empha-sizes: "Using things in your own back yard that are at their peak."

ROD BUTTERS'S **WILD MUSHROOM–CRUSTED CLAYOQUOT OYSTERS WITH ORGANIC GREENS AND ROASTED BEET OIL**

12 Oyster Jim's oysters (or any large West Coast beach oyster)

1/2 cup/125 mL dried wild mushrooms, finely ground (porcinis, morels, lobster mushrooms, etc.)

1/4 cup/60 mL olive oil

1 large bunch salad greens

1 long English cucumber

8 whole chives

2 Tbsp./30 mL roasted beet oil

Remove oysters from shells by boiling, baking, microwaving or barbecuing. Shells will open slightly to allow easy removal of oysters. Set on towel to drain.

Coat oysters with olive oil, reserving some oil for cooking. Place oysters in ground mushrooms, coating each oyster completely.

Put olive oil in a large frying pan over medium-high heat. Gently place oysters in the pan. Sauté on both sides until golden brown, approximately 5-6 minutes. Remove from pan and keep warm.

Slice cucumber into 8 thin strips using a mandoline or slicer. (A sharp knife and a steady hand will also work, but slices won't be as thin.) Arrange 2 cucumber slices on each plate to form a ring. Overlap slices so that their natural juices will hold cucumber together as a "bowl."

Assemble one-quarter of the greens in each cucumber bowl and garnish with 2 chives standing up from each bowl. Arrange 3 oysters on each bowl. Drizzle plates with beet oil. *Serves 4.*

ROASTED BEET OIL

3 red beets, peeled

1/2 cup/125 mL sunflower oil

2 oz./60 g lemon juice

Roast beets in oven till tender, then let cool. Put through a juicer. In a blender, combine beet juice, sunflower oil and lemon juice on low speed. Put oil into squeeze bottle or small container. Use right away or refrigerate.

III. Cooking

I have a friend who lives in a high-rise apartment in New York City. He calls the kitchen "the room with the hot thing in it." The thought of taking raw ingredients and turning them into something palatable, never mind desirable, creates insurmountable fear in him. He has the idea that anyone who cooks competently, without a can opener, is a sorcerer.

At the other extreme, my friends who are acclaimed chefs think nothing of working eighty-hour weeks; managing an ever-changing staff using the most advanced human-relations skills; maintaining a complicated ordering and inventory system; developing recipes that keep food costs in the neighbourhood of 25 per cent of total costs; establishing excellent relations with the food press; innovating sufficiently well to stay ahead of the competition but not the clients; and keeping owners sane and happy. Oh yes—and cooking.

To my mind, neither of these approaches captures the true spirit of food preparation. What cooking has been through the centuries, and should become again, is a means for us to feed ourselves and to feed and spend social time with others. We eat to live, but nourishment is a more complete concept. To be fully nourished is to be fed, loved and cared for—and to have the opportunity to feed, love and care for other people.

A recent survey found that only 10 per cent of U.S. families regularly eat dinner together. Whatever their margin of error, these findings describe a situation that encapsulates much of what is wrong with our society. TV and fast foods have destroyed the joy—and the point—of cooking and eating. But there are signs that this is changing. One of these is the emergence of the Slow Food Movement, which aims to awaken people to the benefits of taking the time to grow or purchase quality food, and to prepare and serve it with respect and caring. Their goal is a return to civility. James Barber, the renowned "Urban Peasant," points out that many "convenience foods" take as much time to prepare as the same product made from scratch. Furthermore, basic ingredients are almost always less expensive and more nutritious than ready-to-eat foods.

Unexpected things happen when people get together to share food, and groups that nourish their members also tend to feed those who come to them hungry. It is harder to be selfish in a nourishing community. The cooks who appear in this chapter understand that concept well, and they know firsthand the importance—and the pleasures—of breaking bread with others.

—H.B.

Karen Barnaby and friend.

🌶 A Lust for Food: Karen Barnaby

Few in the culinary world have such a downright sensual approach to food as chef Karen Barnaby. Even fewer can trace their passion back to eating alphabet cereal in their high chairs. Barnaby's life has mirrored the way Canada eats, from the common-sense dishes of the sixties and the dawning curiosity about ingredients from other countries in the eighties to the contemporary emergence of regional cuisines.

Barnaby grew up in Ottawa eating "the regular food of the time. Roast beef on Sunday, casseroles, peanut butter sandwiches." By the time she was studying Grade 8 home economics, however, she was already wowing classmates with fondue: made, she admits, "with cheddar, and without the wine." She entered the restaurant world at the age of twenty, working at Ottawa's Bohemian Café, where she rustled up quiches, cheesecakes, carrot cakes and hearty soups. Never trained professionally, she has relied increasingly over the years on instinct to make dishes exciting. "Things would just twig me and I'd put them together, such as a winter vegetable soup with sage," she says. Influencing her early on were memories of her grandmothers. One taught her about such "exotica" as zucchinis, eggplants and avocados; the other was "kind of a health food nut," says Barnaby. "I remember eating artichokes when I was no more than five."

Arriving in Toronto in 1981, Barnaby worked with a Thai-Laotian chef who introduced her to the aromatic world of Asian cuisine. Nights, she made cheesecakes at home and sold them to the David Wood Food Shop, then Toronto's most-lauded source of prepared dishes. She ended up working for Wood. Toronto was booming, and customers were avid for new dishes like Thai beef noodle salad and marinated vegetables. Resurrecting her long-time urge to write, Barnaby also coauthored two books with Wood, developing close to half the recipes.

After five years, Barnaby headed south to Cuernavaca, Mexico, for a three-month stint as a private chef. "I was literally in heaven there," she says. "Everything was so fresh. All that fantastic fruit and incredible shrimp." Next stop for Barnaby and her partner and fellow chef Steve McKinley was the West Coast, where she signed on at Capers, a West Vancouver restaurant specializing in fresh, inventive food. From there, she moved to the Raintree, the first Vancouver restaurant to focus purely on a regional cuisine. As the Raintree's executive chef, she opened up North 49, Harvest Moon Café in Victoria and Restaurant Starfish, all places that featured B.C. fish, meat and produce.

Today, as executive chef at the Fish House in Stanley Park, Barnaby aims her considerable talents at fish and seafood: halibut, Copper River salmon, skate, local sole, oysters, clams, mussels, and swimming scallops and prawns when they are in season. Her spare time is just as food-centric. She enjoys preparing whole roasted Dungeness crab bought live from the large Asian supermarket two blocks from her home. Springtime foraging in Lynn Valley on Vancouver's North Shore rewards Barnaby and McKinley with bramble tips to add to salads. Weekend pilgrimages to Vancouver Island can lead to a feast of gooseneck barnacles. Barnaby has also authored several more cookbooks and is the associate editor of a forthcoming book about Canadian women chefs.

Barnaby is modest about being the West's most prominent female chef but far less reticent about the fabulous food available in B.C. She enthuses over "the marvellous strawberries—they're small, sweet, intense in flavour. Raspberries? Same thing." And tomatoes here are "unbelievable," she tells you. But she saves her loudest praise for British Columbia black cod: "I love its sumptuous texture, its melt-in-your-mouth qualities." Barnaby's voice drops—she's lost in pleasurable memory. "I think it's one of the best fish in the world."

KAREN BARNABY'S ROASTED POTATOES WITH GARLIC CHIPS, PECORINO CHEESE AND GARLIC-VINEGAR DIP

These delectable potatoes are finished with a coating of crispy garlic chips and piquant sheep's milk cheese. The garlic and vinegar dip adds a special edge. The success of this recipe depends on how thinly and evenly you slice the garlic.

4 cloves garlic, thinly sliced
1/2 tsp./2 mL salt
1/2 cup/125 mL apple cider vinegar
3 Tbsp./45 mL extra virgin olive oil
12 cloves garlic, thinly sliced
4 medium russet potatoes, washed
salt and freshly ground black pepper to taste
4 Tbsp./60 mL finely grated pecorino cheese

Preheat oven to 350°F/180°C.

To make the dip, combine 4 cloves of garlic and salt in a small bowl. Rub salt and garlic together with your fingers. (Wear gloves if you are shy!) Add vinegar and stir well. Set aside.

Heat olive oil in a small frying pan over medium-low heat. Add remaining 12 cloves of garlic, stirring occasionally until garlic turns golden brown. Do not be tempted to turn up the heat. Immediately pour garlic and oil mixture through a sieve set over a large heat-proof bowl. Drain for 10 minutes. The garlic will become crisp as it cools. Place garlic on paper towels to drain further. Reserve oil.

Cut each potato into 8 wedges lengthwise and toss in reserved oil. Spread potatoes in a single layer on a heavy baking sheet and place on the lowest rack of the oven. Bake for 15-20 minutes, until potatoes are golden brown on the bottom and easy to turn with an egg lifter. Turn potato slices over, season lightly with salt and roast for 15-20 minutes until golden brown on the bottom.

While potatoes are roasting, crush crisp garlic either in a mortar and pestle or by placing it in a plastic bag and crushing with a rolling pin. Mix with cheese.

When potatoes are done, transfer them from the pan, leaving any oil behind, and toss immediately with the garlic and cheese mixture. Season with salt and lots of pepper. Serve with vinegar-garlic dip on the side.

🍃 Isadora's Co-operative Restaurant

Back in the early 1980s there were basically two kinds of restaurants: highfalutin "dining destinations" and spots you could take the kids. Then along came Isadora's, on Vancouver's Granville Island. A friendly, funky place, it not only offered food that was revolutionary for the time but positively welcomed moms, pops and everyone from newborns on up. Something else made Isadora's unusual. As a co-operative venture, it had 1,300 different owners.

The shareholders were people drawn from many sectors of the community: lawyers, educators, activists, social workers, artists—anyone, remembers Patricia Brown, drawn by the line "How would you like to own your own restaurant?" Getting the capital together took two years, says Brown, one of Isadora's founding members and later its accounting co-ordinator. Each $100 share entitled the holder to $25 worth of free food a year. The B.C. Central Credit Union matched $100,000 of the funds raised. A loan from the CCEC Credit Union paid for the leasehold on the building, a concrete-floored shell once used for repairing asphalt equipment, and the restaurant was on its way.

Isadora's opened its doors in May 1983. It was designed as a big open space where kids could play in their own special area while their parents sat at nearby tables. A long, convivial squiggle of a bar made the atmosphere as welcoming to those on their own as to couples and families. Initial plans were to run the place as a worker collective, but the daily challenges of restaurant operation soon led to the more traditional structure of management and staff.

What stayed decidedly different was the menu. "We knew we wanted it to be affordable, healthy and fresh," says Brown. The restaurant's first chef, Hubertus Surm, was determined that the dishes he served be true originals. "We pioneered a lot of things," he says. "Isadora's was one of only two Vancouver restaurants to serve organic meats. We had sushi on the menu. Salmon burgers and vegetarian burgers were both unusual for the time." Isadora's was also among the first to have an open kitchen, to buy salad greens direct from farms and nearby Granville Island Public Market, and to deemphasize meat in favour of lighter dishes. Unique at the time too were salads served as entire meals, with the West Coast Salad—a fixture on many restaurant menus today—including such "exotic" ingredients as mussels, smoked salmon and shrimp.

Isadora's flourished, serving three meals a day. Weekend brunches were popular, and benefits for environmental and community projects were frequent. Corporate connections with charity have now become so common that they're almost considered part of a business plan, Surm points out. "But it was always part of our ethics."

For the first few years, Isadora's went from strength to strength. In 1986, as Vancouver drew global attention with its world's fair, the restaurant received five column inches in the *New York Times*. But witnessing Isadora's growing success, and recognizing that dining tastes were changing, other restaurants began to take a closer look at their surroundings. New eateries specializing in West Coast cuisine sprang up. By the early 1990s, Isadora's faced increasingly strong neighbourhood competition.

In December 1996, Isadora's ran out of money and temporarily closed its doors. "She had reached middle age," says Patricia Brown. "It's a time when you can simply give up, or you can reevaluate." As far as shareholders were concerned, the choice was obvious. They voted unanimously in favour of restructuring, refinancing and reopening. A year later, freshly painted and carpeted, and with plans in the works for further refurbishment, Isadora's was back in business.

While its menu still featured West Coast cuisine, preparations were more "gourmet" this time around. Dishes like halibut with sun-dried tomato and fresh tarragon pesto, or chicken stuffed with spinach and goat cheese, reflected the growing sophistication of Vancouver diners. Seafood chowder, a standard, is a soul-soothing broth of milk and clam nectar dense with salmon, halibut, potatoes and carrots. On other days there might be a tomato three-bean soup or a potage of curried pumpkin. Most breads are baked in house; cranberry herb is much in demand, as are the poppy seed "knot" buns.

Old favourites like the Khatsah'lano burger—salmon and traditional bannock, with cranberry chutney as "ketchup"—and the Go Nuts burger are as popular as ever. Nor has the restaurant's generosity diminished over the years. All profits continue to go to a broad range of social justice and environmental organizations, including Amnesty International, the Western Canada Wilderness Committee, the Nuu-chah-nulth First Nations, the Amazon Rain Forest Fund and Oxfam. Servers still volunteer a portion of their tips to the charity of the month. And, as the menu tells diners, "as part of our philosophy, Isadora's donates funds, food and space for the benefit of community organizations."

These days, Isadora's is doing more than reviving old memories. Friday evening, in the post-dinner hours, is "Songwriter Night," a time for contemporary troubadours to perform their work while diners nibble on appetizers or dessert. Special dinners showcase local salmon and B.C. wine. It's a new approach, and it's bringing in a new generation. But some basics don't change. For those who still dream of owning a restaurant, the price of a share in Isadora's remains at $100.

DRISS HADDIOUI'S **ELDERBERRY BANNOCK**

Driss Haddioui trained in engineering before switching to the world of cuisine. Moroccan-born, he brings what a fellow chef at Isadora's Co-operative Restaurant calls "a lovely sense of spicing" to his foods.

8 cups/2 L white flour
2 cups/500 mL whole wheat flour
3 Tbsp./45 mL baking powder
1^{1}/$_{2}$ tsp./7 mL salt
6 Tbsp./90 mL sugar
6 Tbsp./90 mL butter at room temperature
^{3}/$_{4}$ cup/180 mL elderberries (or other wild berries)
5 cups/1.25 L buttermilk

Preheat oven to 375°F/190°C.

Sift flour, baking powder and salt together. Mix in sugar. Add butter, working into flour with a pastry cutter or fork until butter is the size of small peas. Mix in berries.

Add buttermilk slowly and mix to bring ingredients together. Transfer to floured work surface and knead gently for 1 minute to make a smooth dough. Flatten dough into a uniform 1"/2.5 cm thickness. Cut into small triangles.

Place on oiled baking tray and bake for 8-12 minutes, or until golden and puffed. *Makes 24 portions.*

❢ Community Kitchens

Take a group with something in common, add a kitchen facility—in a church basement, a local centre or a school—bring in ingredients and mix well. That's the thinking behind community kitchens, and judging from their success across the country, it's an idea that's right for the times.

Give a man a fish and he will eat for a day; teach him to fish and he will eat for a lifetime, says Andrea Taylor, until recently community kitchens co-ordinator for Vancouver. An adult educator with a B.Sc. in Dietetics from the University of British Columbia, she first branched out into community kitchens in Kamloops, through the Kamloops Home Support program. When she began in 1993, there were two kitchens on the go. Taylor ran ads and produced a brochure. Word of mouth did the rest, and by June 1995, when she decided to move back to Vancouver, Kamloops had "thirteen full-fledged running-like-crazy groups." Today, there are even more.

Former Vancouver community kitchens co-ordinator Andrea Taylor (at back) and her team display their homemade preserves.

Community kitchens originated in Peru, Chile and Guatemala in the 1970s, says Taylor. "Generally they were, and still are, groups of women getting together every day to prepare the evening meal." Inspired by a visit to Peru, a group of Montreal women launched their own kitchen. There are now about three hundred community kitchens in Quebec alone, and the movement has fanned out across the country. In Vancouver, a grant allowed community nutritionists and the Food Bank to start a community kitchens program, and eventually a strong partnership was established with BC Gas.

Community kitchens, says Taylor, can operate anywhere there's a stove, a sink and a good-sized countertop. "People eat better, their kids eat better," she maintains. "Cooking together can be a first tentative step into community life that leads to awareness of other services, to school or a job."

At Vancouver's Frog Hollow community kitchen, children are the only common element. While their parents cook in the biweekly Multicultural Cooking Club, small babies look on and rambunctious eight-year-olds use an outside step as a Stairmaster. Communal cooking is nothing new in cultures where two or more generations live together and women often do not work outside the home. Tonight sixteen families have shown up, and ten nationalities are represented.

Each family pays $2 per member, and all cook the foods of their homelands. Frances Yao, from Indonesia, puts the finishing touches on gado-gado, a traditional salad of sliced cooked potatoes, hard-boiled eggs, green and red pepper strips and broccoli flowers. Jaywa Chang has made salt-and-pepper chicken, a dish from her native Taiwan. Jolanta Kupczyk, who is Polish, is busily tossing a heap of fried noodles and greens. Annette Chia from Singapore is en route to a bridal shower but has dropped in because she enjoys the camaraderie.

At an arborite table, two generations sit making wonton. Joyce Tan has lived in Vancouver for seven years. Her father, Pan Ying Wei, speaks no English and moved here from northern China only a month ago. Hugh Tan, husband of Joyce, acts as translator for those who want the recipe: pork, ginger, green onion, soy sauce and water. "I never add water: now I know why my wonton are dry," says a woman from another part of China, explaining that "even though we are all ethnic Chinese, sometimes we can't all speak the same language. China itself is multicultural."

Around the province, community kitchens come in all shapes and sizes. Four young mothers get together each week to prepare several days' worth of dishes while one of them keeps an eye on all the children. A group of women on welfare hold a regular canning session, earning a little extra income by selling their salsas, pickles and jams at farmers' markets and also using the opportunity, as one points out, to give something back to supportive neighbours and friends.

Preparing food with others is one of the most potent pleasures of being human. A community kitchen co-ordinator can be anybody who enjoys organizing and being with people. In the couple of years he's been a group leader at Barclay Manor, a West End seniors' centre in Vancouver, Ivor Parry has shown participants more than 150 dishes. He leafs through his binder of recipes, some hand-written, others photocopied from magazines: chicken cacciatore, Vietnamese salad rolls, lasagna, fudge, fish chowder, curry, Mexican meatballs and Edmonton Klondike beans—"That's a favourite of ours."

"Albóndigas, too," says Parry. "Some people didn't like all the chili peppers."

Rain or shine, every Thursday the Barclay Bread Burners—up to a dozen men in their seventies and eighties—get together to cook lunch. Jack Duguid offers his beef stew recipe, one his mother made when she and his father were homesteading. He recalls his own early days in B.C.'s Cariboo region, when each fall he'd buy fifty pounds of beans. Every Sunday he'd cook up a six-quart pot of them and, since fourteen-hour days in the orchard left little time for cooking, he'd eat from that all week. Raised in an era when stewing beef could be had for nine cents a pound and eggs for twenty-nine cents a dozen, the Barclay Bread Burners can't bring themselves to pay an arm and a leg for an entrée, but they are nervous about the standards of cleanliness in cheaper eateries. Culinary independence is a far better option.

Here today as a guest, Andrea Taylor answers questions. Acidophilus milk is good to drink, she says, if you are taking antibiotics. Floyd Williams minces parsley. Beside him, Dick Cardy, a little slower since his recent stroke, intently chops onions. While the soup simmers, Parry points out that an upcoming seniors' event will conflict with the cooking session. No contest. "People on their own often don't feel like cooking or eating," says Taylor. "A major life change when you're a little older can shock you so much that you stop caring about eating properly."

Conversation turns to the move from a rural to an urban lifestyle, to the loss worldwide of agricultural land, to the inequality of food distribution and climbing food costs, rent and taxes. In ten years' time, the Barclay Bread Burners figure, none of them will be able to afford to live in their long-time neighbourhood.

The mushroom and barley soup is so thick you could stand a spoon in it. The bread is a touch heavy but tasty and filling. Food costs, when you cook as a group, are minimal, and at the end of the session, as always, everyone drops a loonie in a white china bowl.

During lunch, participants share information on supermarket specials, with Parry gleefully pitting Save-On's deals against Safeway's. Shopping wisely is just one of the skills that people who attend a community kitchen may learn. Guidelines are mutually agreed on, says Taylor. Do participants want to eat together? Is anyone vegetarian, or allergic to a specific food? All this and more is discussed, along with such down-to-earth details as bringing your own containers—and, as in any kitchen, who will volunteer to do the dishes.

SWEET AND SOUR LENTILS

This recipe was made by the Jubilee House Community Kitchen for World Food Day in 1997.

3 cups/750 mL lentils, rinsed
6 Tbsp./90 mL vegetable oil
3 medium onions, chopped
2-3 red or green bell peppers, seeded and diced
2-3 winter squash, diced (try zucchini if making in summer)
5 cups/1.25 L sweet apples or pears, chopped
shredded ginger to taste
vinegar to taste
6 Tbsp./90 mL light soy sauce
6 Tbsp./90 mL brown sugar
6 Tbsp./90 mL ketchup
2 Tbsp./30 mL Tabasco or other bottled hot sauce
1 1/2 tsp./7 mL ground black pepper
1 Tbsp./15 mL cornstarch

Cover lentils in water and cook for about 20 minutes, or until tender. Drain.

In a large saucepan, heat oil and add onion, pepper and squash. Sauté for 7 minutes. Add apple and ginger and cook for 2-3 minutes more.

Add lentils, vinegar, soy sauce, sugar, ketchup, hot sauce and pepper, and cook over medium heat for 15-20 minutes, stirring occasionally.

Combine cornstarch with an equal amount of cold water in a small bowl. Whisk cornstarch mixture into lentils, reduce heat and cook for 5-10 minutes more. Serve over rice. *Serves 12.*

SANDRA HAINLE'S **CELLAR DWELLER'S PASTA**

Sandra Hainle is an organic vintner in B.C.'s Okanagan. The grape harvest, which begins at the end of September and continues throughout October, is a time of clear cool air, brilliant sunshine and work, work, work. Hainle finds that robust "comfort" foods, usually prepared in one pot, are unusually satisfying then.

1 head green cabbage (small to medium)
2 tsp./10 mL salt
8 oz./250 g broad egg noodles
2 Tbsp./30 mL vegetable oil or bacon fat
1 medium onion, diced
1 red pepper, diced
1 green pepper, diced
2 cloves garlic, minced
1 Tbsp./15 mL Hungarian sweet paprika, or more to taste
2 Tbsp./30 mL poppy seeds
2 Tbsp./30 mL dark maple syrup
3 Tbsp./45 mL low-fat sour cream or light cream
freshly ground black pepper
green onion, minced, for garnish
chopped toasted walnuts, for garnish

Finely shred cabbage and place in a colander. Toss with salt and let sit for at least 30 minutes, or until it begins to soften. Rinse thoroughly in cold water and squeeze out all excess moisture. Set aside.

Cook egg noodles according to package directions, drain and set aside.

In a large, heavy skillet or Dutch oven, heat oil or fat and sauté onion, red and green pepper, and garlic until soft. Add cabbage, paprika and poppy seeds and continue sautéeing until cabbage is lightly browned. (You can splash in a bit of wine at this point if you've got it handy.) Add noodles, maple syrup and cream, turn heat down, and stir until heated through. Season with black pepper to taste. Add a bit more cream if noodles seem dry. Garnish plates with chopped green onion and walnuts.

Serves 4 hungry working types or 2 slightly piggish types.

❦ Whistler à la Carte:
Bernard Casavant

Sharing the pure deliciousness of local cuisine is a constant mission for chef Bernard Casavant.

Listing your forte as "regional cuisine" is easy enough if you're the chef of a small restaurant in a rural setting. It's harder if you're cooking for hundreds rather than dozens, and considerably more so if, instead of being ringed by gardens and orchards, your restaurant backs onto a ski slope. Challenging? Yes. But chef Bernard Casavant proved that it wasn't impossible.

By the time he was hired to head up the kitchen at the Chateau Whistler Resort in 1989, Casavant had already cut his teeth at Vancouver's Expo 86. There, as executive chef at the Canadian Club, he showcased local food for visiting royalty, heads of state and movie stars. Moving to Vancouver's Four Seasons Hotel, he found a climate equally keen on nurturing local farmers.

Casavant faced two major problems in Whistler: a lack of employees and a lack of suppliers. The first he solved by instituting an apprenticeship program that skimmed off the cream of British Columbia's emerging generation of chefs. Apprentices were instilled with Casavant's belief that banquet food should be every bit as imaginative and tasty as that served in the resort's Wildflower restaurant. They also learned about the importance Casavant placed on the organically grown ingredients he was slowly amassing from a small band of local producers.

Driving around back roads had brought Casavant to some farms; word of mouth took him to others. Often there were surprises: a farmer might sell him tomatoes, then produce a bunch of fresh thyme. Among his most exciting discoveries were Terry Berry Organic Farms, whose certified organic Black Angus beef is monitored from start to finish, and Lillooet Lake Herbs, owned by Lori and Fraser Ternes. Casavant began to invite the Ternes to the Wildflower each November for a working dinner. He would illustrate how a squash might show up roasted and teamed with lemon thyme in a soup, while its seeds, roasted with the Ternes' "ring of fire" chilies, would be inserted under the skin of a pheasant prior to roasting. He and the couple would go through seed catalogues, debating what was feasible to grow and what was overly labour-intensive.

Meanwhile, the Chateau Whistler's reputation for organic cuisine was growing. A typical dinner at the Wildflower might begin with sweet, fleshy local tomatoes paired with sun-dried olives in a herb-scented pastry case. An entrée of home-smoked salmon that had been steeped in maple syrup and brown sugar was accompanied by grilled pine mushrooms collected in the surrounding woods. Dessert would draw on both Asian and B.C. flavours via a green cardamom parfait served with wild huckleberry compote. In the tastiest way possible, Casavant was spreading the word that what was raised locally was a catalyst for world-class cuisine.

He was also connecting producers and consumers even more directly by becoming a driving force behind a weekly farmers' market in Whistler. On any given Sunday, locals and visitors would stop by to pick up big bunches of bottle-green chard, small local melons, red and white radishes, honey, and homemade crêpes and cookies.

In 1996, with the already large Chateau Whistler poised for more expansion, Casavant opted to open his own place, a small café right next door. "At Chef Bernard's we are adding style to take-out dishes by using the freshest ingredients," says its owner. "Everything is local." Casavant serves simple sandwiches, home-baked breads and legendary soups, including his well-known roasted carrot and Brie. He has also developed Ciao Thyme, a line of oils, vinegars and dressings. "I'm 100 per cent Canadian and proud of it," he says, "and there's no use in being proud of where you live if you don't walk the talk."

BERNARD CASAVANT'S **WARM CORNBREAD AND QUINOA PUDDING WITH TOMATO COULIS AND ZUCCHINI PUREE**

CUSTARD

1/2 cup/125 mL skim milk (plus 1 Tbsp./15 mL)

3 Tbsp./45 mL canned evaporated milk

1 whole egg

1 egg white

3 garlic cloves, minced

pinch pepper

1/2 cup/125 mL quinoa, cooked

1/2 cup/125 mL cornbread, day-old and cubed

1 Tbsp./15 mL shallots, peeled and sliced

2 Tbsp./30 mL red and green peppers, diced

3 Tbsp./45 mL mozzarella cheese, shredded

2 Tbsp./30 mL fresh thyme

vegetable oil spray

Combine skim milk, evaporated milk, whole eggs and egg white in a large bowl. Combine garlic, pepper, quinoa, cornbread, shallots, mozzarella, peppers and thyme in a separate bowl. Pour liquid over top and lightly mix.

Spray timbale moulds or ramekins with vegetable oil spray. Fill carefully, tamping each timbale. Poach in a 170°F/76°C water bath until set, about 20-30 minutes. Remove from oven and keep warm.

TOMATO COULIS

2 roma tomatoes, blanched, peeled and seeded

1 Tbsp./15 mL shallots, peeled and sliced

pinch pepper

1 Tbsp./15 mL water

Place all ingredients in a blender and purée until smooth. Stain through a sieve. Keep at room temperature.

ZUCCHINI PURÉE

1 cup/250 mL zucchini, trimmed and seeded

2 Tbsp./30 mL spinach, cleaned

2 Tbsp./30 mL soft tofu

1 garlic clove, roasted

pinch pepper

Cut zucchini into slices. Blanch both zucchini and spinach briefly. Place in blender with remaining ingredients. Blend until smooth and bright green. If too thick, thin with heated water.

Unmould "puddings" carefully and place one in the centre of each plate. Drizzle tomato coulis over top and pipe zucchini purée around the edge. Garnish with a sprig of thyme. *Serves 4.*

❦ South Vancouver's Sikh Temple

From the ritual of Holy Communion to a Salvation Army soup kitchen, almost all religious movements emphasize the link between physical and spiritual nourishment. At the Sikh Temple in South Vancouver, this link is made in a very practical way. Here anyone—not just those of the Sikh faith—can partake of the dishes served twenty-four hours a day in the *langar*, or food hall.

Outsiders are quickly made to feel at home. Women are encouraged to cover their heads, and all guests are instructed to wash and dry their hands; a smiling woman in a traditional *salwaar kameez* mimes the action, then points to a stack of compartmentalized plastic trays and invites guests to help themselves.

At a large serving table, men spoon out curried potatoes and cabbage, savoury dal, tiny chickpea balls in buttermilk and, for dessert, noodles in a thick, sweet, cinnamon-scented sauce. With the rhythm and speed born of long practice, another man folds chapatis and sets them alongside the other food on guests' trays. Men and women tend to eat separately. Children play quietly on the floor. Weaving together the conversation and the clang of kitchen pots are half-sung, half-spoken readings from the Guru Granth Sahib, the scriptures, relayed in from the prayer hall.

Most Sikhs come from the Punjab in northern India, the area that feeds much of the country. Farmers are highly respected there, and here, in their adopted country, many are farmers and farmworkers still. Being part of the land, they will tell you, is part of being Punjabi. Observant Sikhs donate a certain percentage of their wages, or its equivalent in goods or service, to the temple.

Many bring in sacks of onions, potatoes and other produce grown in the rich soil just outside Vancouver. Others volunteer to work in the kitchen, a task considered visible service to the universal spirit.

Volunteers at a long table in the kitchen are making the traditional bread called roti, nipping off small amounts from a large mound of dough and rolling each one into a thin, flat disk. At the

12'-long grill, more helpers flip the roti as it develops its characteristic black spots. A man dabs each piece of bread with butter as it comes off the grill, than stacks it neatly in a cloth-lined picnic cooler. In the communal kitchen, the giant pots and pans—each one at least a yard across—bubble and steam as, measuring by eye, an "uncle" (a term of respect for an elder) adds a ladleful of spices, then stirs the seasonings in with a giant wooden *musandha*. Work is nonstop. All dishes are freshly made two or three times a day.

It is usual for those attending a temple service to eat from the same pot with neighbours and family afterwards, and anyone organizing a celebration is welcome to cook here as well. Following a wedding ceremony, guests eat in the langar before attending the official reception. And, just as food and worship are intertwined, religion and social life also intersect. Seniors stop by the temple to meet and chat, others to learn of marriageable sons and daughters or jobs available. For those in need, there is counsel and consolation. Newborns are brought directly from the hospital to the temple to be blessed before they are taken home.

Meeting place, shared kitchen, focus of spirituality—and guarantee that no one will ever go hungry for food or company—South Vancouver's Sikh Temple is truly at the heart of its community.

🥕 Green College

Students at Green College enjoy exceptional cuisine thanks to food and beverage manager Ian Cowley.

For most of us, the words "institutional food" conjure up images of bland sauces and unexciting casseroles. Compare that with the fare at the University of British Columbia's Green College. In high summer, dinner may be a barbecue offering a choice of red pepper patties or game hen with garden rosemary and garlic, with seasonal fruit and berries for dessert. In fall, diners can sit down to Quebec quail roasted with chanterelles, cranberries and toasted pine nuts, or to a wild mushroom, goat cheese and polenta tart with fiddlehead ketchup, followed by Okanagan pears poached in red wine and vanilla. To coincide with the release of Beaujolais Nouveau, the college presents a week of French-inspired cuisine using local ingredients in late November. Even in early January, when regional produce is limited, the dinner can be B.C. fallow venison and potatoes roasted with juniper and garlic.

By any standards, Green College is unusual. Founded in 1993 as a centre for advanced interdisciplinary scholarship, it brings together students from around the world. Built on the cliff tops of Vancouver's Point Grey, overlooking Howe Sound and the coastal mountains, the college buildings centre on Graham House, a 1912 mansion that has been extensively renovated to accommodate its new role. Its entire second floor houses the Great Hall, an impressive wood-beamed room that is a central feature of life at Green College. Here students come together twice a day not just to eat at the three long tables but to share ideas and good company. Academic and artistic programming is often scheduled around the dinner hour.

The task of feeding more than a hundred people twice a day is the responsibility of the Green College Dining Society, a nonprofit organization. The society also handles catered functions, preparing five- or six-course dinners for up to 150 people. "The meal plan is run on a break-even basis," says food and beverage manager Ian Cowley. "Catering is at market rates. Surpluses are fed to the students."

Cowley defines the cuisine prepared by his chef and staff of five as "elegant home cooking." Dishes are different every day, not only for novelty's sake but because residents eat here five days a week. As well as offering foods that are tasty without being high in fat, menus must meet the needs of the 30 per cent of students who are vegetarian, as well as those on special diets. Reflecting the diverse origins of the diners, food celebrates American Thanksgiving, Jewish holidays and other special days in the calendar. The college is licensed to sell wine and beer with meals, and their selection is often from B.C. vineyards and microbreweries.

What Green College students get, says Cowley, is "really interesting food at cost." Diners also benefit from their food and beverage manager's illustrious past, which includes positions with the Four Seasons Hotel in Calgary and Vancouver, two years at Claridge's in London, and three years in France at two- and three-star Michelin restaurants.

His travels have left Cowley with a fervour for top-quality regional ingredients. Whenever possible, he uses produce grown without chemicals or pesticides. "Organic apples are twice as expensive, but worth it," he maintains. He points through the window of his stone-walled office at what was once a covered swimming pool. Today it contains garden plots where residents and staff grow beans, peas, sweet potatoes and other vegetables for use in the kitchen. An adjacent greenhouse produces fresh herbs.

Cowley is an enthusiastic member of Xclusively B.C., a non-profit organization that raises funds through dinners and other events to provide scholarships and bursaries to British Columbians pursuing a career in the culinary arts. In all things food-related, says Cowley, "I want to see more homegrown."

IAN COWLEY'S **GRAPE AND WILDFLOWER HONEY TART**

PASTRY

2 cups/500 mL pastry flour
1 cup/250 mL unsalted butter, softened
4 egg yolks
1 egg white
1 cup/250 mL sugar

Combine ingredients and lightly knead (or mix with a dough hook) until very smooth in texture. Add more flour if mixture becomes too sticky. Refrigerate at least 1 hour, or preferably overnight.

TART

1 large bunch seedless grapes, de-stemmed, washed and dried
1/4 cup/60 mL wildflower honey
olive oil
sugar

Toss grapes in honey and allow to soak for at least 1 hour.

Divide pastry in two. Roll out and line an oiled 10"/25 cm tart pan. Place a layer of grapes on pastry base and fill any gaps with smaller grapes. Roll remaining pastry and use to cover tart. Crimp edges to seal. Brush with olive oil, sprinkle with a little sugar and bake at 350°F/180°C for 20-25 minutes, or until brown and crisp. Best eaten while still a bit warm. *Serves 4-6.*

IV. Creating

You've eaten as much as you can reasonably eat of the fruit and vegetables you harvested from your garden, and there are still leftovers. You have a strong craving on a December night for a juicy piece of fruit, and you remember the home-canned peaches you bought in August at a roadside stand in the Okanagan Valley. Ah! In the heart of winter, what better way to relive the euphoria of the harvest than to open a container of a truly superior product and experience the smell and taste of the season in which it was grown. Cheese-making may have started as a way to preserve milk in a convenient form. Wine may be just another form of preserved juice. But clearly both are more than that. Processing creates food items significantly different from the original ingredients that go into making them.

Today, when supermarkets have just about anything we desire anytime we want it, why make or buy preserved foods? Some obvious reasons come to mind, among them keeping food costs down, ensuring top quality and putting together personal, meaningful gifts. For me the answer includes these things but goes further. It can be a deeply satisfying experience, one that sates body and soul, to eat the fruit of a plant at the peak of its perfection. Anticipation of spring asparagus or autumn corn heightens our pleasure when it finally arrives on the table. Having our fill, then letting go until the appropriate season arrives again, helps keep us in harmony with the rhythms of nature.

Buying from local processors is the next best thing to making it yourself. Since even small-scale commercial processing is almost always more lucrative than farming or fishing, primary producers will often supplement their incomes by "adding value" to their goods. These so-called cottage industries are usually also a labour of love, a demonstration of commitment to quality over quantity and an expression of caring for the local ecology. Contrast this to the huge transnational food organizations that take a product and turn it into something that is expensive to buy and costs a fortune to advertise. Corporations will spend $70 to $90 million just to introduce a new breakfast cereal that, by their own admission, contains nutritional value only when milk is added. So does the cardboard carton!

We get real value and nourishment from our food budget by buying local products, whether fresh and in season or preserved in some way. Taste is also a primary consideration, of course, and as you'll see in this chapter, the wine, cheese, balsamic vinegar and other food items produced in British Columbia are second to none.

–H.B.

❦ The Pleasure of Preserves: Duncan Holmes

Food consultant, writer and keen amateur chef Duncan Holmes has a 50' x 20' allotment garden in the suburb of Richmond, just outside Vancouver. It costs him $40 annually and repays him with not only fresh vegetables almost all year round but the raw materials for a dazzling array of pickles and relishes.

Like most gardeners, Holmes finds his zeal sometimes results in excess crops, and he often intentionally grows enough to put by for months when his garden is dormant. "I do have a lot of beets at the end of the season," he says, "but beets *ordinaire* are not for me." Instead, he turns them into pickles, sometimes spicing ordinary vinegar with a splash of balsamic or apple cider vinegar as well. White onions, red onions and red cabbage are also pickled, and Holmes is especially proud of his recipe for saffron-flavoured shallots. "Sometimes I'll deliberately make my preserves look pretty," he says; he occasionally enters his progeny in local contests and took "best of show" at one fair for three years running. At home, stacks of his brilliantly hued jars serve as the focal point at the end of a hallway.

Squash and pumpkins show up in relishes, as does zucchini, notorious for its profligate ways. "I have zucchini relish from my early childhood," Holmes jokes. "It makes a wonderful Christmas gift."

Duncan Holmes in his allotment garden.

Left:

Remember when the only tomato was a red tomato? Today not just yellow but orange, pink and deep crimson varieties are increasingly seen at farmers' markets.

Below:

Untainted by pesticides, the grapes at Hainle Vineyards in B.C.'s Okanagan are made into top-quality wines.

Bottom:

Sampling British Columbia's unique regional cuisine is a delicious experience for visitors from around the world.

Top left:
Spicily scented basil flourishes at Andrew Yeoman and Noël Richardson's Ravenhill Farm on Vancouver Island.

Top right:
Originally a secret family recipe, Donna Denison's Little Creek Dressing has found an eager audience around the province.

Left:
A fund-raiser for FarmFolk/CityFolk held annually at Fraser Common Farm, Feast of Fields lets attendees chat with chefs and nibble a salad grown only yards away.

Above:
The bounty of local farms is showcased at urban food events like Stone Soup, held every spring in East Vancouver.

Far left:
Just in time for Hallowe'en: pumpkins for the pickin' in B.C.'s Fraser Valley.

Left:
Dazzling colour and peppery flavour make nasturtiums a popular pick for a vase—or a salad.

Left:
Providing an edible link between farm and city, Organics to You brings weekly boxes of seasonal produce right to the door of a growing number of Vancouver residents.

Below:
Tasty lemon cucumbers and monster zucchinis thrive at Ravenhill Farm on Vancouver Island.

Above:
Sun-warmed and straight off the cane: that's the way to eat raspberries.

HUBERTUS SURM'S **PICKLED PUMPKIN**

6 cups/1.5 L vinegar
3 cups/750 mL water
2 1/4 cups/560 mL sugar
3 Tbsp./45 mL coriander seeds
1 tsp./5 mL salt
1/2 tsp./2 mL cinnamon
3/4 tsp./3 mL whole cloves
6-8 lbs./3-4 kg pumpkin, peeled and cut into 1/2"/1 cm cubes

Combine vinegar, water, sugar and spices in large pot. Bring to boil. Add pumpkin and cook until barely tender. Cool in liquid. Store covered, in refrigerator, for at least a couple of days before using. Keeps for weeks. *Makes 6 pints/3 L.*

A Lifetime of Preserving

Duncan Holmes

Maybe it was because we were poor, or because we wanted to capture the seasons in nonrefrigerated times. Maybe it was because there was always an abundance in summer of good things that preserving became a ritual of our family life back then in forties Australia. Apricots and peaches were givens. We did them in Fowler jars that involved tricky rubber bands, lids and clips. My father was a master at getting the fruit to stack up beautifully in the jars before we poured in the syrup and started the processing—on a wood stove that in the heat of summer burned like the fires of Hell. I went back to Australia not too many years ago, and we opened with great ceremony the last of some pears that were preserved in 1927. They were delicious!

All of this stuff was kept on shelves in a cellar beneath the kitchen. We got at it by moving the kitchen table to one side, lifting a wooden lid and heading on down the stairs by flashlight to the dank little room below. It was a fascinating place that served its purpose well, and a great place to hide.

Canning is a process that combines need, opportunity and the chance at some future date to savour the tastes of times and seasons past: "Remember when we picked this?" Vegetables in season come fast, and no matter how many friends and relatives you have, you can't consume or give away everything a garden can produce. At any one time, I have a couple of hundred jars of stuff that's ready to use, give away or enter in a show.

I take a great deal of care in my canning, using only the very best ingredients. While I check recipes each season to make sure I'm stocked with basics like sugar and vinegar, whatever happens after that really depends on what else is in the cupboard. I've added saffron to pearl onions, grenadine to peaches, fresh ginger to pears, rum to apricots. All of these things and more make exotics of the ordinary, not to mention the fact that they look wonderful when they're displayed.

For freezing, I tend to make lots of food in one pot, which preserves all of the flavours in a much better way. That delicious leek and potato soup can be trotted out for a special occasion dinner or an ordinary Monday night.

ANDREW SKORZEWSKI'S **GOOSEBERRY RELISH**

"It's a given for me," says chef Andrew Skorzewski when he's asked about the role that fresh, local vegetables play in his highly rated cooking. "I believe in letting ingredients speak for themselves—and when they're fresh and organic, it's so easy." The passion for good food that he has explored in Montreal, Toronto, Stockholm and Vancouver extends into his private life too. "We live a block from the East Vancouver Farmers Market," he says. "We buy organic vegetables there not just for ourselves but also to make food for our one-year-old. We want to give her the best."

This relish will keep well for a month in the refrigerator. You can also can it, following instructions for jams or jellies and processing in a hot water bath for 20 minutes.

2 cinnamon sticks
1 1/2 tsp./7 mL whole allspice
1 tsp./5 mL coriander seed
1/2 tsp./2 mL cloves
2 whole star anise
zest of 1 orange
cheesecloth
1 1/2 cups/375 mL water
3 cups/750 mL granulated white sugar
1 1/2 cups/375 mL vinegar
5 lbs./2.25 kg gooseberries

Tie spices and orange zest in cheesecloth. Combine water, sugar, vinegar and spice bag in a non-corrosive pot. Bring to a boil and add gooseberries.

Simmer for about 20-30 minutes, until gooseberries start to thicken. Remove from heat and proceed with canning or cool and transfer to a container and refrigerate.

❦ Salt Spring Island Cheese Company

For its size, population and varied terrain, Canada is a land of shamefully few cheeses. Cheddar, Oka . . . even the most ardent fromageophile finds it hard to name half a dozen, and the most revered cheeses, the Bries and Camemberts and Stiltons, are imports from thousands of miles away. By comparison, France produces some five hundred varieties, infinitely more if you include the locally made and unnamed types found at every village market. But there are hopeful signs this side of the Atlantic. Part of the emergence of regional cuisine is the resurgence of local, artisan-made cheese.

One of the biggest draws at the Saturday market on Salt Spring, the largest of B.C.'s southern Gulf Islands, is cheesemaker David Wood. Locals and visitors alike crowd around his small, umbrella-shaded table to taste samples, to chat and to get into fierce discussion. 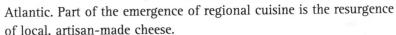 What shall it be this time around? The Saint Jo, an unctuous Camembert-style sheep's milk cheese, or a fresh, tangy goat cheese to serve with a crisp green salad? And how about the aged, more pungent goat cheese? Because it's so difficult to decide, most people end up buying all three, and some of his yoghurt too.

For David Wood, meticulous care leads to exceptional cheeses.

Drawn by the island's bucolic setting, Wood, a cookbook author and former owner of a specialty food store in Toronto, moved to the West Coast in 1990. He was aware of the growing demand for gourmet cheese, and he had heard of the cheeses that were starting to be produced in Vermont and California. He knew too that Salt Spring sheep were renowned for their quality.

Wood and his wife, Nancy, purchased a number of Arcotts, hybrid sheep bred by, and named after, the Agricultural Research Centre in Ottawa. "Melting pot sheep," he calls them. "One that was thrown in was Friesland. It's the best dairy sheep but only available in Canada very recently." Learning to make cheese, he says, was trial and error, his only training a five-day course at Washington State University in

Spokane and a week's study-tour in Corsica. His equipment came from a goat dairy that was about to close down.

The flock today numbers over sixty sheep, each yielding about two cups of milk a day. In 1996, Wood also began producing goat cheese, obtaining the milk from a farm on Vancouver Island. The 130 gallons he processes each week translate into 330 pounds of cheese.

Drain, salt, dry, ripen: cheese-making techniques have changed little through the centuries. In Woods's dairy, the milk is first pasteurized for thirty minutes at 145°F, which kills off all bacteria. Once cooled, it is transferred into a stainless steel vat. Culture—the bacteria needed to make the cheese—and coagulant are then added, changing the milk into curds

and whey. Fresh goat cheese rounds stand in their moulds for three days. Some are marinated in oil and basil, others have sky-blue borage or other edible flowers carefully applied to their surface. Drying the cheese calls for lower temperatures and humidity. A small room off the dairy is cooled to 12°F, and it is there the distinctive "bloom" of mould develops. Round Saint Jo cheeses drain in small baskets whose vertical slits provide signature ridges. Square Explorers—a traditional French aged goat's milk cheese—ripen for two weeks. (Two months is normal, says Wood, "but we haven't been able to hold onto them long enough.") Wrapped and refrigerated, the cheeses are ready to market.

David Wood indicates a corner of the dairy he has set aside for experimentation. Here he is attempting to make a hard cheese with sheep's milk. He envisages other cheeses, too. In his view, "a blue made from sheep's milk could be even better than Cambozola." Making cheese is like making wine, Wood will tell you. "Any fool can ferment grape juice. But making something that is good and repeatable is a different story."

KAREN BARNABY'S **TEA-SCENTED FRESH GOAT CHEESE**

"You can experiment with different teas in this recipe," says Barnaby. "My favourite is Genmai Cha Japanese green tea with roasted barley and rice. The nutty flavour of the grains and green tea complement the cheese beautifully."

4 oz./125 g soft, unripened fresh goat cheese
2 Tbsp./30 mL fragrant tea leaves, dried (divided into 2 portions)
cheesecloth

Wrap cheese in a single layer of cheesecloth with very little overlap.

On a piece of plastic wrap large enough to wrap the cheese, spread 1 Tbsp./15 mL of tea in a band lengthwise down the middle. Place curved edge of cloth-covered cheese in tea at one end of plastic wrap and tightly roll in the wrap, making sure that tea is fully covering the sides of the cheese. Place cheese with one flat side up and sprinkle half the remaining tea over it. Twist the end closed tightly. Repeat on remaining side. What you should end up with is a piece of cheesecloth-wrapped cheese that is almost completely covered in tea and wrapped tightly in plastic. Refrigerate for 24 hours. The longer cheese is marinated, the stronger tea flavour becomes.

Remove plastic and cheesecloth from cheese and discard. Serve.

ROD BUTTERS'S **LAYERED YAMS AND BEETS WITH GOAT CHEESE**

3 large yams, peeled and sliced thinly
3 large beets, peeled and sliced thinly
1 whole leek, cleaned and sliced thinly
$1/2$ onion, peeled and sliced thinly
3 cloves garlic, minced
3 Tbsp./45 mL fresh tarragon (or 1 tsp./5 mL dried)
4 Tbsp./60 mL soft goat cheese, crumbled (or your favourite cheese)
2 cups/500 mL whipping cream
salt and black pepper to taste
non-stick spray or oil

Preheat oven to 350°F/180°C.

Spray baking dish with non-stick spray or oil. Spread yams on bottom layer of pan. Sprinkle with one-third each of leeks, onion and garlic.

Sprinkle with one-quarter tarragon and goat cheese and add one-half of cream. Season with salt and pepper.

Cover with layer of beets, and repeat the process with the other ingredients, alternating layers of yams and beets. You should have at least two layers of each. Finish top layer with remaining goat cheese. Pour remaining cream over top.

Bake for about 45-60 minutes, or until a knife easily pierces the vegetables. *Serves 6-8.*

❦ Venturi-Schulze Vineyards

When immigrants leave their homelands, they bring with them more than their memories. They bring their traditions, especially those linked with food. Dishes are not precisely the same in a new setting, of course. A North American tomato is not identical in flavour to a tomato raised in England: climate and soil—the combination known in the vineyard as *terroir*—are subtly different. Recipes too evolve and change. The cooking of seventeenth-century France becomes Québécois cuisine. Asian ingredients are borrowed by western chefs to add fragrance and flavour to local fish and meats. But sometimes the techniques required to create a much-loved casserole or condiment are so rigorous that immigrants rarely attempt to transplant them. Such is the case with balsamic vinegar.

Work is constant in Marilyn Schulze's vineyard.

The balsamic vinegar found on supermarket shelves may be made from wine vinegar, concentrated grape juice, and caramel or juniper berries. *Genuine* balsamic vinegar, complex in flavour and hauntingly aromatic, comes only from a handful of producers in Modena, Italy—and from a winery on Vancouver Island, where Marilyn Schulze and Giordano Venturi meticulously recreate the slow miracle that transforms ripe grapes into a dark, mysterious essence.

Born in the Australian outback, Schulze is a microbiologist. Venturi, a former electronics teacher, comes from Spilamberto, nine miles south of Modena. By the time the couple met in 1986, Venturi had already been experimenting with making his own balsamic vinegar, using grapes from his quarter-acre suburban garden. "You just didn't do that in Italy," he says. "In the old days, only the nobility made balsamic vinegar." Equipped with an authentic culture from an Italian *acetaia* (a place where vinegar is made), he started a barrel for his two sons. It takes at least twelve years for the vinegar to develop its characteristic rich, sweet flavour and stained-glass deepness of colour. Venturi checked

on it occasionally, but mostly he left nature to get on with its work. When marriage to Schulze added her son and two daughters, and later the couple's daughter Giordana, to the family, the pair resolved to start a barrel a year, one for each child.

By now, home was a fifteen-acre spread on southern Vancouver Island, five acres of which they had planted with vines. They experimented with different varietals, honed techniques and soon made the Venturi-Schulze label one of the most sought after in the Pacific Northwest. It is also one of the most unusual. Bottles are capped instead of corked, and wines are given evocative names like Essence of Millefiori or No. 3 (inspired by a wine that Venturi first tasted in Italy while listening to the third concerto of Bach's Brandenburg Concertos). Through-out it all, at the back of their minds was the thought of making balsamic vinegar commercially.

It's a painstaking process. Simmered in a stainless steel boiler over a wood fire, the grape juice—organic, unlike in Modena—is first reduced to half its volume. It then goes into "nursery" barrels—standard wine barrels—before beginning a journey through a series of five barrels each made from a different wood: cherry, chestnut, ash, acacia and Italian oak. "Cherry gives a rich sweetness. Chestnut has depth of colour and a good evaporation rate," says Venturi. "Each one imparts its own fingerprint to the vinegar." Evaporation over the twelve-year period reduces the juice by 90 per cent. Barrels are arranged in rows in descending order of size—50, 40, 30, 25 and 20 litres—and eventually the smallest barrel of all holds thousands of dollars worth of vinegar.

A National Research Council grant in 1994 enabled the two to study different strains of bacteria and the role that temperature played in the vinegar-making process. Obtaining authentic barrels from Italy involved considerable time and infinite patience. Even though Venturi was fluent in *spilambertese*, the local dialect, it took repeat visits, numerous phone calls and several years of negotiation before the barrels were shipped to Canada.

Although Venturi-Schulze does not advertise (indeed, does not even have a sign outside their winery), word of mouth—and a mention on *Good Morning America*—means that the one thousand bottles of balsamic vinegar released every so often sell out almost immediately.

It's not making the couple wealthy, and nor are their wines. They've learned that while hard work and meticulous vineyard management can do much, they are powerless against such climatic swings as the heavy rains of 1997, which ruined 70 per cent of their crop. But they remain enthusiastic. "We're not aiming to be rich," says Schulze. "We want to make a living—and we will. That's a wonderful use of five little acres of land."

Giordano Venturi and Marilyn Schulze drape their vines in netting to protect the grapes from birds.

Using Balsamic Vinegar

Lovers of food treat authentic balsamic vinegar with the respect this rare ingredient deserves. In Italy, drop by valuable drop, it may be sparingly drizzled on boiled meats and is often sprinkled sparsely over ripe strawberries. At their winery on Vancouver Island, Giordano Venturi and Marilyn Schulze often add a little homemade balsamic to prawns or asparagus. Executive chef Michael Noble at Diva at the Met in Vancouver, the only mainland restaurant to carry Venturi-Schulze wines, likes to experiment.

"Venturi-Schulze balsamic has the characteristics of wine," says Noble. "With other balsamics, the aging process can often take away the flavour of the grape. This has a really fresh, almost floral taste to it." Convinced that "it would be sacrilege to just use it in a vinaigrette," he surmises that "it might be wonderful in marinated seafood or in a sauce for chicken." Meanwhile, he uses the intricate essence primarily in desserts, and then only for special occasions. In a show-stopping finale at a winemakers' dinner in 1996, Noble topped an anise-scented shortcake with local berries marinated in a tiny bit of balsamic; more of the precious substance was swirled into concentrated strawberry purée to create a superb sorbet.

ANDREW SKORZEWSKI'S **CHARRED ASPARAGUS AND RADICCHIO SALAD WITH BALSAMIC VINEGAR AND PARMESAN DRESSING**

2 cloves garlic, sliced
1/2 tsp./2 mL salt
2 Tbsp./30 mL Dijon mustard
4 Tbsp./60 mL balsamic vinegar
1/2 cup/125 mL olive oil
ground black pepper to taste

1/2 lb./250 g asparagus
1 head radicchio
1/4 cup/60 mL parmesan cheese

Mash garlic with salt. Place in a stainless steel mixing bowl along with mustard and balsamic vinegar. Slowly whisk in olive oil. Season to taste with a little black pepper. Set aside.

Preheat a grill or cast-iron pan to very hot. Snap tough ends off asparagus. Place asparagus on grill or in pan and cook, turning until each spear is charred on all sides. Remove and cool. Cut into bite-sized chunks.

Tear radicchio into a mixing bowl. Add asparagus and parmesan cheese. Ladle in about 4 oz./125 g of dressing and toss. *Serves 4.*

♥ Little Creek Dressing

Donna Denison (left) introduces customers to her savoury salad dressing.

Never underestimate the power of a favourite family recipe. Donna Denison's salad dressing has such an addictive flavour—tangy and nutty at once—that sales have climbed to the point where what was once intended as a small home business now steers the direction of the family farm.

The land that Denison and her husband, Dale Ziech, own, a twenty-five-minute drive northwest of Kelowna, B.C., was originally part of her great-aunt and great-uncle's property. When it was subdivided among the four Denison brothers and sisters in 1984, Donna and Dale found themselves with six fairly level acres at the end of a long and winding road, bordered by Okanagan Lake and backed by forest. They called their new operation Little Creek Garden.

Donna was a potter, and Dale had been an orchardist since the age of twenty. They built their own house on the land, bartering plumbing for Ziech's tree-pruning skills and using recycled materials. In 1986, Denison gave birth to twin daughters, Kerisa and Amber.

Denison initially worked "out" to support the farm, where Ziech was growing organic vegetables in raised beds—eight or ten tomato varieties, strawberries and baby vegetables, as well as edible flowers, which they sold to local restaurants. Casting around for a home-based business, Denison found it in the dressing the couple regularly drizzled over their homegrown salads. She mixed up a jar and contacted the nearby Summerland Research Station, a federally run resource that helps people to develop and refine food products. By July 1995, Little Creek Raspberry Vinaigrette Dressing was ready to roll.

Dale Ziech's organically grown tomatoes find a ready market in the Okanagan.

Inside the bottle was a mixture of oil, lemon juice, raspberry vinegar, fresh farm-grown basil and garlic, and tamari; the dressing also has "a secret ingredient," which the label reveals as nutritional yeast. At first, Denison used vinegar made from her own farm's raspberries, but when sales exceeded supplies, she turned to certified organic raspberry concentrate supplied by local farmers.

How to Use Your Favourite Salad Dressing

- Use as a marinade/basting sauce for grilled fish, chicken, meat or tofu.
- Add to pita pockets filled with fresh organic mixed greens for a simple, delicious snack or lunch.
- Use instead of butter or margarine on steamed or baked vegetables.
- Make a wrap using herbed soft tortillas spread with hummus, fresh organic mixed greens and salad dressing.
- A quick sauce can be created by sautéing some fresh organic tomatoes in dressing and adding freshly chopped basil and freshly ground pepper or cayenne. Cook down lightly and serve on your favorite pasta, or on rice.

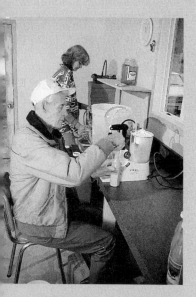

Donna Denison joins forces with her father, John Denison, to bottle Little Creek Dressing.

She first set up operations in the commercial kitchen of a local resort hotel, then shifted to the Girl Guide camp of which she is caretaker. Today, Denison runs her business from a small cabin close to the farmhouse, once intended as a pottery studio. "I try to put love, light and good energy into the dressing," she says, "and I feel I can do that here on the farm." In 1996, she acquired a bottling machine, and she now produces ten cases of dressing an hour. With very little marketing, she sells through health food stores, craft shows, produce stores and food stands. Local restaurants and the neighbouring Hainle winery also use Little Creek Dressing on their salads.

The product's success has helped Denison and Ziech to refocus. "My philosophy in modern farming is flexibility," says Ziech. "You have to lead the market, see potential. Our goals are changing all the time." He continues to grow strawberries and tomatoes, has added echinacea (which he sells to a local processor) and has seeded his land plus three more leased acres with fourteen different types of lettuce, kale and other greens. More garlic and basil plants will be grown this season, and the raspberry patch has been considerably enlarged. Explains Ziech: "Instead of more cash crops, we're going into processing products that support Donna's salad dressing." Donna is looking to diversify as well. Over the next few years, she has plans to add black currant and salal berry vinaigrettes to the Little Creek Dressing line. Not bad for a product that started out in her family kitchen.

❦ Hainle Vineyards Estate Winery

With a successful vintage largely dependent on the fickle variables of sunshine, temperature and rainfall, making wine has always been a labour of love. Making *organic* wine with all its attendant restrictions, as Okanagan Valley winemakers Tilman and Sandra Hainle do, demands extraordinary passion and a resolution to work with—rather than against—nature.

Wanting to live on a piece of land untainted by harmful chemicals is one of the reasons the Hainles have chosen this route. Their urge to minimize the environmental footprint created by agricultural and business activity is another. But above all, the couple is eager, as Sandra writes in their newsletter, "to make good wines which are as pure as possible."

The perception that organic agriculture leads to a politically correct but inferior product is put to rest by the Hainles' enviable track record of awards and acclaim. Theirs was the first B.C. ice wine to

Sandra Hainle checks grapes for quality.

Organic Certification

Alyson Chisholm, Certification Review Subcommittee, B.C. Association for Regenerative Agriculture

Organic certification assures the consumer that food labelled "organic" has been produced according to a certain set of standards. To improve soil phosphate levels, for example, an organic farmer may use bone meal, bird and bat guano, and hard and soft rock phosphate, but not superphosphate or organophosphates. The standards also regulate the quality of water used in production, the management of soil, the fair treatment of farm labourers, and the conditions under which livestock is raised.

A grower who wants to apply for organic certification must first become a member of an accredited certifying body and then submit a map of the farm, including the fields or yards surrounding it; a description of the farm's production history, crop and soil management plan; and a record of farm inputs (seeds, seedlings, fertilizer, livestock, packaging materials, and products used to control disease, insects, animal pests and weeds). Soil management, production and sales records must also be accurately maintained.

It is common for farms to be inspected at least twice a year during the first three years, the first inspection scheduled with the farmer and the second unscheduled. The farmer pays for each inspection.

An inspector does the following:

1. Carries out a visual inspection of the farm.
2. Takes samples of soil and water to be analyzed. Soils are tested for levels of pH, nitrogen, phosphate, potassium and other minerals.
3. Checks the areas adjacent to the applicant's land and buildings. If the organic farm is surrounded by conventionally farmed land, railways, roads, water courses or industrial or farm buildings, then a buffer zone must be present. This is to ensure that nonorganic materials, such as

attract serious attention, and their 1987 vintage alone has won seven gold medals. "We realize that not all of our customers are particularly looking for organic wines; they may be choosing our wine just because they like it," says Sandra with understandable pride.

The Hainle connection with wine goes back to the early seventies, when Tilman's parents moved the family from Germany to a piece of land just north of Peachland, where they planted a vineyard for their own use. Soon the venture had grown way beyond a hobby, and in 1980 the Hainles started making wine in commercial volumes. Tilman returned to Germany to study wine making. Back in Canada, he married Sandra, a practising lawyer who joined the winery in 1989.

The following year, the Hainles started the move towards organic production. In one way at least, nature is on their side. The sandy soil of their vineyard provides great drainage—"It's soil that wriggles between your toes," says Sandra. It's also soil that is too dry and light for the vineyard scourge of phylloxera to take hold. Spraying with silica gel prevents mildew, and composted chicken manure is used as fertilizer, but otherwise the Hainles try as much as possible to work in line with the vineyard's own ecosystem.

Walking between the rows of Traminer and Riesling vines, Sandra points out how these natural systems work. "The first thing you'll notice is a lot of what we call 'volunteer plants'," she says. Others might call them weeds and eradicate them with herbicides to create a picture-perfect vineyard that would be "neat, tidy and probably toxic." But volunteers have their advantages. Though they may occasionally crowd out young vines, they also provide cover to prevent moisture loss and create a home for beneficial insects. The Hainles' solution to overeager volunteer plants? Mowing them down periodically and digging them into the ground, where they help to condition the soil.

Hereabouts, the wildlife is abundant and occasionally invasive. Deer visit the vineyard daily but leave it untouched, mainly, Sandra believes, because "we leave so much green for them." But nothing, not even a recorded tape of a dying bird, will keep the starlings away, and the sound of cannons—another popular remedy—frequently echoes down the valley. More of a problem are the bears that clamber down the hillside and can go through two hundred pounds of grapes in a night, tearing bunchs off with their paws for the ultimate teddy-bears' picnic. The most effective solution would be an electric fence around the property—a prohibitively expensive proposition for now, as are the nets that would foil starlings.

Fighting off insects is almost as challenging. A tiny light-green bug, the Virginia creeper leafhopper, is a particular nuisance, sucking the juice from vine leaves and weakening the plants. The Hainles rely on predatory wasps as their first line of defence; as a last resort they use an insecticidal soap that is naturally derived and allowed under organic standards.

Another of the challenges of engaging in organic agriculture is the fact that "there's a lot of confusion out there about what is and isn't organic," Sandra explains. "We're still the only winery in B.C. and perhaps even Canada to have both our vineyards and our processing certified organic, and we're the only winery that has wines bearing the COABC [Certified Organic Associations of B.C.] label. There is a tendency to say that a wine or a winery is organic when organically grown fruit is used; however, you can take organic fruit and apply a lot of technology and chemicals that are not in line with organic standards at all. We've gone the extra step and had our processing certified."

Close to 60 per cent of the Hainle portfolio is now organic wines. Why not all? Because, like many wineries, the Hainles need more grapes than they can produce themselves to be commercially viable. These must be purchased, and at the moment there is simply not enough organically grown fruit available.

To team with their wines, the Hainles grow organic foods in their garden, where eighteen raised beds produce enough herbs, edible flowers and salad greens to supply the winery's Amphora Bistro during the growing season. In this airy, tiled space adorned with works by local artists, the menu is strong on ingredients from neighbourhood suppliers. Chef David Forestell's signature dishes include asparagus and leek soup, beer-braised free-range chicken, and roasted root vegetable and bulgur salad. Locally baked bread is a constant, as are greens drizzled with locally produced Little Creek Dressing. The Hainles have recently added labels from other wineries to their list, including raspberry, black currant and red currant dessert wines that hail from the Fraser Valley.

pesticide sprays or chemical fertilizers, will not contaminate the organic fields by air or water.
4. Writes a report and presents it to the farmer.

The decision to grant a farm transitional status is made by a certification review subcommittee. Transitional status will last for three years: the time required for the farm and farmer to make the transition from conventional to organic production. After this three-year period, if all standards are being maintained, the farm will be granted certified organic status.

The certification process is ongoing, as new products are evaluated and new information is released about products previously assumed to be "safe." For example, until the "Mad Cow Disease" (BSE) outbreak in the United Kingdom, the use of blood meal as a quick-release nitrogen fertilizer was common practice. Certifying agencies are now restricting the use of blood meal fertilizer imported from countries that are BSE-endemic.

There are currently many regional certifying bodies in B.C. All are members of the provincial co-ordinating association, the Certified Organic Associations of British Columbia. COABC maintains provincial standards developed in conjunction with regional groups, and a certifying agency wishing to join COABC must adopt these standards as the minimum to be achieved. Recognizing how important the bioregional context is in certifying organically grown food, COABC certifies growers primarily through local certifying agencies.

Lunch and a glass of wine. That's the small picture. The big picture, as Tilman and Sandra Hainle are aware, is their vineyard's place in its surroundings. "We highly value the fact that only eighteen acres of our thirty-acre parcel is cultivated," says Sandra. "The rest is left in its natural state, full of wildflowers, ponderosa pine, and native shrubs and grasses. We see ourselves as stewards of this natural heritage and have tried to step lightly upon it. The landscape includes the vineyard; the vineyard does not exclude the landscape."

Tilman Hainle uses a refractometer to check the sugar level in grapes.

SANDRA HAINLE'S **SALAD DRESSING WITH DESSERT WINE AND DRIED FRUIT**

1 cup/250 mL dried berries or other dried fruit, diced small
1/3 cup/80 mL dessert wine (this can be a really decadent way to use that leftover ice wine
    or sweet sherry)
2 Tbsp./30 mL balsamic or fruit vinegar
2 Tbsp./30 mL dark maple syrup to taste
herbs to taste (lemon thyme is very nice)
1/4 cup/60 mL extra virgin olive oil
salt and freshly ground black pepper

Combine dried fruit and dessert wine in a small, non-reactive saucepan and bring to a boil. Remove from heat immediately, cover and let sit for at least 30 minutes, or until fruit is rehydrated. Some liquid will remain in the pan.

Combine vinegar, syrup and herbs in a bowl, add fruit and remaining liquid from saucepan, and mix. Whisk in oil until emulsified. Season with salt and pepper. *Dresses enough greens for 4 people.*

JOHN BISHOP'S **RED WINE AND ELDERFLOWER SORBET**

1 cup/250 mL elderflowers
6 cups/1.5 L red wine
3 cups/750 g sugar
3 1/2 cups/850 mL water
1/4 cup/60 mL glucose

Add elderflowers and red wine to a saucepan over medium heat. Reduce to one-third. Remove from heat and let steep.

In a heavy stainless steel pot, mix sugar, water and glucose and bring to a boil, stirring occasionally. Skim off any scum that forms on the surface. Boil for 3 minutes.

Mix sugar syrup with red wine and let sit overnight in the refrigerator.

Pass through a sieve. Freeze in an ice-cream maker, following manufacturer's directions. *Makes 6 cups (1.5 L).*

❦ Chocolate Arts

The wrapper on a typical candy bar tells you exactly what it contains: sugar, glucose, modified palm and vegetable oils, unsweetened chocolate, modified milk ingredients, cocoa butter, mono and diglycerides, and a few other multisyllabic substances. The truffles, bars and individual candies that Greg Hook produces for his Vancouver store, Chocolate Arts, are made of simpler stuff. Like pure chocolate. And sweet butter. And whipping cream. What also makes Hook's creations unique is that his chocolate shells often enrobe local, organically grown fruits.

A pastry chef before he turned full time to chocolate-making in 1992, Hook was always knocked sideways by the clarity, punch and colour of fresh fruit. "We have the most gorgeous blueberries in British Columbia," he says. "I dehydrate them and use them like raisins in chocolates. Or I soak them in Galiano liqueur and make a filling with them." Also dried for use are biodynamically grown local peaches so juicy that, says Hook, "you have to get a bib to eat them."

Apart from organic orange and lemon rind from California, raisins and a handful of nuts not native to B.C., everything comes from local farms. Never mind that unsprayed hazelnuts are more expensive than imports. They taste sweeter, which is why Hook prefers to use them in his hazelnut truffles and Cleopatras—single chocolate-dipped hazelnuts encased in chocolate pyramids. Each summer, he sorts through four hundred pounds of organic cherries that will be dried before being coated with chocolate or soaked in rum for Christmas treats. Over the summer months, local strawberries and

Greg Hook demonstrates his artistry.

raspberries are concentrated into intensely flavoured purées and later made into fruit leather.

"What we're trying to achieve are world-class chocolates," says Hook. The look of the chocolates is very much a part of that, he adds, which is why he has trouble creating a piece that is merely solid chocolate—it is just too plain. Swirls of light and white loop across the surface of an Easter egg. Each heart-shaped Raspberry Passion chocolate is decorated with white chocolate banding.

On a table stands a tray of shiny chocolate leaves. "Chocolate takes on the shine of any surface it's put on," says Hook. "That's one of the magic things about it." He's constantly beguiled by this substance and the skill required to work with it, a skill, he says, that takes at least three years to learn. "Getting the feel of the chocolate is important. You're using all your senses."

On the other side of Hook's long, narrow kitchen, one of his five staff works at the tempering machine, filled with 52 pounds of dark, viscous, satiny chocolate. "Tempering is having the chocolate properly crystallized," Hook explains. "That's what gives it snap, crunch and a nice gloss, and helps it unmould properly." Hands in the air, he sketches the chemical changes that take place. Thinner than mechanically produced varieties, each shell at Chocolate Arts is made by hand. Hook cuts a finished chocolate in half to reveal that top, bottom and sides are completely even. "The difference between too thick and too thin is a fraction of an inch."

Despite his fondness for filled chocolates, Hook is best known for chocolate creations inspired by West Coast aboriginal art. In his store's early days, he was looking for original ways to use his chosen substance. "Initially we were going to do after-dinner mints with fresh mint," he remembers. Thinking creatively led to a brain wave. What if some of Haida artist Robert Davidson's work could be reproduced?

"I immediately thought of red, black and white, the traditional colours of Haida art, as milk, dark and white chocolate," says Hook. He approached Davidson, who was enthusiastic. The initial piece, in the shape of a frog, was drawn directly from a jewellery mould. Subsequent designs of a moon and a killer whale were reproduced as both chocolates and jewellery. Staying true to the original design was problematic initially. Most chocolates are straight-sided or slope slightly from top to bottom so that they can pop easily out of rigid plastic moulds. The Davidson chocolates have a slight overhang, which required the design of rubber moulds (at a cost of $250 each) that could be flexed in either direction. The six indentations in each mould are first hand-painted with a thin layer of chocolate, then filled with more. Constant vibration gets rid of tiny air bubbles that can lead to pin-prick flaws in the finished piece. Once hardened, the edible works of art are wrapped individually or packaged in a pine box with local hazelnuts and dried organic blueberries.

Right now, Hook has his eye on apricots as a potential ingredient. There's no question that offbeat flavours are one of his chief claims to fame. The Romeo, a pairing of blackberry creme and blackberry truffle filling, is a best-seller. Rhubarb Rhapsody features that astringent fruit. Available only during the month of October, his autumnal truffles combine a spiced pumpkin purée with chocolate and nuts. He'd like to marry chocolate with pear or with apple.

There are too many ideas and not enough hours in the day, says the chocolatier. As far back as 1989, he was experimenting with herbs in chocolate, an idea a little ahead of its time, he acknowledges. Recent samplings of raspberry and thyme leather, and tarragon wafers encased in dark chocolate, have been received far more positively. Maybe now his market is ready.

GREG HOOK'S **CHOCOLATE SAUCE**

Use good-quality imported chocolate for this recipe. I recommend Valrhona,
a French variety, as it transforms any dessert it's used in from "great" to
"exceptional."

1 cup/250 mL whipping cream
3/4 cup/180 mL dark chocolate, chopped fine

Bring whipping cream to a boil (be careful as cream will expand and tends
to overflow the pot). Pour over chopped chocolate. Mix until chocolate
melts and a smooth sauce forms. May be done ahead of time and reheated.

If sauce separates (i.e., it looks as if there is oil on top), the cocoa
butter has come out of the chocolate. Just boil a small amount of whipping
cream and add in small amounts until the mixture comes together.

Making Apple/Plum Fruit Leather

2 cups/500 mL apples
2 cups/500 mL plums
1-2 Tbsp./15-30 mL honey or maple syrup

Cut apples and plums in half, remove cores and pits, and chop coarsely.
There is no need to remove the peel. Purée fruit in a food processer or
blender, adding honey or maple syrup. Spread purée evenly, in a layer
about 1/4"/.5 cm thick, on a tray lined with plastic. Dry.

A commercial or homemade dryer is ideal for making fruit leather,
but not necessary. If you are drying in your oven, use a fairly heavy piece
of plastic to line a cookie tray. A large freezer bag cut in half works well.

The key to drying in an oven is to keep the temperature at the lowest
setting possible: 250°F/120°C or less. Since it takes 18 to 24 hours to dry,
you may want to leave fruit in overnight. Check several times a day, and
rotate fruit if it is not drying evenly. The fruit leather is ready when it is
not too sticky but still pliable. It should peel easily away from the liner.

Fruit that is properly dried should keep indefinitely in a dry, dark place,
but the best place to keep it is the freezer; cut leather into serving sizes,
roll these in plastic wrap and then place in a freezer bag.

Fruit leather is wonderful alone or mixed with cereal, and it is a good,
quick energy boost when hiking. For a special treat, dip one end of rolled
leather into chocolate.

V. Marketing

A dairy producer once told me about a farm tour she had hosted for a local school. She went all out, showing her visitors everything from grass seed being planted, cows grazing, the compost heap being maintained and manure tea being sprayed to fertilize the grass, on to the barns and the milking and finally to the truck taking the milk to the dairy. At the end of the tour, a teacher asked to speak to the farmer alone. "This was the most interesting and educational class trip we've taken," she said. "There's just one thing I wonder about. You work so hard—why don't you just buy milk from the store the way I do?"

I passed this story along to an urban Grade 7 teacher, who told me another. "We were assigning a class project," she said, "and as part of it I asked one of my students to go to the supermarket and buy some butter. 'Where do I find it?' the student asked me. 'In the dairy section,' I said. 'What's that?' he asked. It turns out he had never been in a supermarket. His parents both worked and were too busy to take him shopping. They bought convenience foods almost exclusively and ate in front of the TV."

Today, most of the food on North American tables has travelled great distances—an average of 1,500 miles—to get there. The many hands this food passes through make it difficult, if not impossible, for the consumer to learn much about what went into producing that food. Food labels, as a source of reliable information, are laughable. When our food is coming from distant, unknown sources, we can only hope that the marketer is cautious, diligent and ethical.

Buying locally allows us to check these things out for ourselves. Home delivery services, farmers' markets and Community Supported Agriculture (C.S.A.)—in which the food buyer purchases shares to support the farmer in advance of the coming season's harvest—are among the fastest-growing sectors of the food industry. Connecting with the grower reduces worry for the eater, but that's not the only reason these services are so popular. Many consumers are also beginning to realize how much fun it can be to buy their food directly from the people who grow it.

By the same token, many farmers understand that they have much to gain by educating and involving the end-of-the-line consumer. They can get more immediate and sympathetic feedback that way, and with this information they can better meet market demands. Establishing a more direct relationship allows producers to reap some of the profits that ordinarily go to as many as four or five middle organizations. And farmers who market directly are also forming closer ties with one another to better co-ordinate product availability and reduce the social isolation many have experienced.

The people profiled in this chapter are all dedicated to supplying urban dwellers with products that were in the ground only hours before. In doing so, they are providing some of the freshest, best-tasting, most nutritious and most beautiful food available anywhere on earth.

—H.B.

🥕 Straight off the Land: Krause Brothers Farms, Hazelmere Farm and Sudoa Farm

In a time when the chilled perfection of supermarket fruits and vegetables is accepted as normal, it's often hard to remember that "farm-fresh produce" was once something more than an advertising cliché. Yet today, many British Columbians are finding ways to reconnect with local farms and food producers so that the berries, the lettuce and the potatoes they eat are once again right off the land.

An hour's drive from Vancouver's city core is the fertile Fraser Valley, where the names on the mailboxes—Krause, Dreidiger, Erikson—tell a tale of the Europeans who settled here, drawn by a soil that promised fruitful harvests.

Henry Krause and his brother Alf grew up on a poultry farm with a large garden. "We went out and picked berries when we were kids," says Henry. He laughs. "We hated it then. *For sure*, I wasn't going to be a farmer." But the Krause family's next home, a property with strawberries growing on it, piqued the brothers' interest, and gradually agriculture became their full-time profession. Today they farm 170 acres of fruits and vegetables. Some of it is sold to local stores; much of it goes straight into the hands of the consumer.

The reasons why city types make the journey to Krause Brothers Farms are several, says Henry Krause. "It's an outing, a day in the country, a chance to spend time on a farm and get fruits and vegetables as fresh as they can be." Price is also a consideration: buying direct from the producer means lower cost.

June at the farms brings a rare opportunity to savour the intense flavour of locally grown strawberries. High sugar content means a short shelf life, explains Henry, so supermarkets prefer varieties with longer life spans. The first crop of the season, the fresh strawberries grown at Krause Brothers Farms are deeply scarlet and full of juice that invariably runs down your chin. The Totem and Rainier varieties are harvestable only for a scant three weeks, so, since 1990, the Krauses have experimented with ever-bearing types; they now have seven acres of these under production. Next in line for a turn in the spotlight are Chilliwack, Meeker and other varieties of raspberries, followed by blueberries and Loch Ness blackberries—so-called, says Henry, "because they're real monsters."

The variety of produce available at the farms has grown tremendously over the years, as has consumer interest. Cucumbers, corn, musk melons and peppers are all popular. In 1994, the brothers started growing artichokes, which now fill three-quarters of an acre. While their farms are not certified as organic, the Krauses are slowly moving away from conventional growing. Henry's wife, Edith, a biologist, keeps an informed eye on the bug population, and the farms practise integrated pest management using ladybugs and other insects to get rid of caterpillars. "Monitoring them lets us be more selective when we spray," says Henry, "and that happens as little as possible."

Not all Fraser Valley growers have farming in their blood. The Kings are a good example: Gary once owned a commodities company and Naty was a foreign exchange broker. It wasn't just the idea of green spaces that made them switch professions. It was their four small daughters. "We wanted to be able to feed our children properly," says Naty. In the Kings' book, that meant no overprocessed foods

filled with chemicals, a cause, they believed, of one of their daughter's allergies. They purchased land in 1984 and three years later Hazelmere Farm was selling its first organic produce, tasty vegetables grown in soil fed by cover crops, compost and manure from local farms. Their first customers were wholesalers and a single Vancouver restaurant. Before long, farmgate sales added to their market.

The Kings' most recent venture is a one-stop shopping outlet based at the farm. Through arrangements with other Lower Mainland growers and suppliers, Hazelmere is able to offer their 150-strong customer base, all people who live in the farm's immediate vicinity, virtually everything they are likely to want, from Fuji apples and red Bartlett pears ("gorgeous!" is the appended note on a sample list faxed to clients) to sixty types of vegetables, including cylindrical red or golden beets, burdock and jewel yams. Free-range eggs and organic yoghurts and cheeses can be found in the dairy section. There are grains, nuts, pastas, frozen vegetarian pizzas, sorbets, and organic flours and grains, as well as fresh black bean dip, B.C.–made fruit spread, pancake mix, pasta sauce and eight types of organic breads. The list has mushroomed as customers take advantage of prices uninflated by the usual store overhead.

Veggies are picked to order, Gary explains, which cuts down on handling. "We don't have to harvest unless it's being sold that day. The disadvantage of most farmgate sales is that, at the end of the day, wilted vegetables have to go on the compost heap."

The Kings have devoted fans among Vancouver's culinary professionals. For the past eight springs, Dennis Green, now executive chef at Bishop's, has leafed through seed catalogues with the owners of

Hazelmere Farm. "It's so important getting top-quality stuff," says Green. "With wholesalers, you don't always know what variety you'll be getting. Take beets; there are about fifty different varieties that could be grown." By working with the Kings, Green can specify which type of vegetable he wants and when he wants it harvested. For a chef, it's like having a living larder. The produce comes to the restaurant twelve hours out of the field. "And once in a while, we'll come up with something really strange," Green says, mentioning the Emperor tulips that the Kings grew for him some years back. He used the petals in salads.

"I really want to feed people, not just provide fancy things," says Gary King. Take carrots, for instance. "Commercial carrots are grown for transportability, easy mechanical harvesting and long storage life. They don't break when dropped eight feet into a truck. A Nantes-variety carrot shatters because it's so crisp."

Dropping into a farm to see what's available or shopping by fax are two of the ways food lovers can get close to the sources of their food. Community Supported Agriculture (C.S.A.) is another. The concept of C.S.A. is generally thought to have originated in California, but it may have its roots in Europe. At one end of the spectrum, C.S.A. shareholders actually own a farm and have control over the crops grown there. The more typical practice is for subscribers to pay a certain amount to a farm at the start of the growing season, which entitles them to a weekly supply of produce delivered to a central pick-up point until the harvest is complete. "It's good to follow the rhythm of the earth and the growing cycle," says one subscriber. "Mother Nature gives us these leafy greens early in spring as a kind of cleanser. As the months go by, it seems natural to move to root vegetables."

Sue Moore and Anne Warren of Sudoa Farm describe their system as "modified C.S.A. We're also an economically viable market garden, selling to stores and to a wholesaler." They have put a cap of twenty on their C.S.A. customers, because they can only transport a certain volume of produce to the farmers' markets in Vancouver, Coquitlam and Kamloops where the boxes are delivered.

Do-It-Yourself Berry Picking

1. Call ahead before you visit to make sure the farm is open and the picking is good. Ask which size of container to bring.

2. Park where indicated. Even if it looks as though there are closer parking spots than those marked, these may be thoroughfares for farm vehicles and delivery trucks.

3. Weigh in at the fruit stand so that you won't have to pay for the weight of your container, and ask where to pick. The people at the stand can give you some good tips.

4. Stay in the row you're assigned. It's better for you and better for the grower if the field is picked through systematically. That way you won't find pockets of rotting berries left from the last pick. If there aren't many berries in your row, pick what there are, then ask to be assigned to a new row.

5. Try to pick all the ripe berries. The small ones taste just as good as the big ones.

6. Should you bring your kids? That depends on how old they are, and how many berries you plan to pick. If you're on a family outing and you only want enough berries for dessert, of course. If you need 200 pounds for a year's supply of preserves, probably not, unless your kids are old enough to be of real help. Some farms have a small play area for children, but it is usually only designed to entertain kids for a short time. Please watch that children don't trample on the plants or pick in other people's rows.

7. Sampling is allowed, but use common sense. Growers have a lot more invested in their produce than a grocer does; their profit margins are slimmer and they're only open for business for a few months. One berry farmer in Manitoba has a sign in his field that says, "Eat a berry, pull a weed."

8. If you phone in an order for picked berries, collect them when you say you will or call in plenty of time to cancel. That way your order can be sold to someone else that day.

9. If you can, pick in the morning, when there are lots of berries and the air is still cool.

Early in the season, boxes will be crammed with green onions, radishes, salad mix, herbs, spinach and rhubarb. By summer, it's beets, carrots, new potatoes, early cabbage, broccoli, cauliflower and the last of the peas. At the end of the season, winter squash, red and green cabbage, green beans and "storage" potatoes take pride of place. Ten of Sudoa Farm's 126 acres are devoted to vegetables; the remainder are hay fields, pasture and wood lots.

The subscribers' cost—$320 for a couple, $500 for a family—is literally seed money. Sudoa Farm guarantees a minimum of twenty weeks' delivery, in good summers more. Vancouver customer Eva Riccius can't say enough about the quality of Sudoa Farm's products. "I remember this amazing garlic; some of it I actually replanted in my garden. Another highlight were little yellow pattypan squashes so sweet that we often just sautéed them with butter and garlic." She raves about the "more intense flavours and deeper colours" of organic vegetables, adding, "I prefer it when they're oddly shaped. When vegetables are all the same size and colour like they are in the supermarket, it freaks me out."

Riccius is also enthusiastic about the personal relationship that she and her four housemates have built with the farm. "We went and stayed there last Labour Day," she says, "and if you want to go work there for a week, you can do that, too. Anne and Sue are great people. It's nice to know who's looking after your vegetables."

ASSEFA KEBEDE'S **LENTIL AND ONION STEW**

Self-taught in the culinary arts, Assefa Kebede learned his technique from his aunt, a famous chef in his native Ethiopia, and his spice-blending skills from his mother. Kebede first introduced Vancouverites to the lusty curries and subtle grain dishes of Ethiopia in 1987, and the following year saw the launch of his Nyala Ethiopian Restaurant. These days—a reflection of Kebede's explorations of African cuisine—his restaurant is known as the Nyala African Hotspot. And these days the herbs and grain he needs are specially grown for him in the Fraser Valley.

Berbere is the basic spice mix for cooking Ethiopian stews.

BERBERE

3 Tbsp./45 mL cayenne pepper
3 Tbsp./45 mL Hungarian paprika
3 Tbsp./45 mL Spanish paprika
1 tsp./5 mL ginger powder
1 tsp./5 mL bishop's weed (ajwain)
1/2 tsp./2 mL cloves
1/2 tsp./2 mL cinnamon
1/2 tsp./2 mL cardamom
1 Tbsp./15 mL salt
water
vegetable oil

Mix all dry ingredients in a food processor. Keep in powder form in a tight container. For stews, mix berbere powder with water until it becomes a paste. Put in a jar, add a quarter-inch layer of vegetable oil and refrigerate.

STEW

4 cups/1 L red lentils
8 cups/2 L water
3 cups/750 mL onions, peeled and diced
1/2 cup/125 mL oil, divided
1 Tbsp./15 mL ginger, minced
3 Tbsp./45 mL tomato paste
3 Tbsp./45 mL berbere paste
salt to taste

Wash lentils and soak for 10 minutes. Heat over medium-high heat for 20 minutes or until soft but not mushy. Drain and reserve.

Heat a pot over medium-high heat for 30 seconds. Add 1 Tbsp./15 mL oil, onion and ginger, and cook until onion browns. Add remaining oil, tomato paste and berbere. Add lentils and continue cooking, stirring constantly until mixture is warmed through. *Serves 4-6.*

10. Strawberries will stay fresh longer if you leave the hulls on. However, if you are taking berries directly home to make jam or to freeze them, removing the hulls as you pick will save you time.

11. If you can't process or eat berries right away, they must be refrigerated—don't leave them in the garage overnight! Raspberries, which are especially perishable, have a shelf life of twenty-four hours at best even with refrigeration. Strawberries and blueberries will last a bit longer, but the sooner you use them, the better the flavour.

VIKRAM VIJ'S **CAULIFLOWER RICE PILAF**

At Vikram Vij's Vancouver restaurant, called simply Vij's, Indian food goes way beyond traditional curries. Since 1994, European-trained Vij and his wife, Meeru, have earned a stellar reputation—and numerous awards—for ground-breaking fusion cuisine that combines local ingredients with centuries-old techniques. The restaurant even has its own garden, a long narrow space where Vij grows herbs for garnishes and experiments with Indian varieties such as the curry leaf.

1 cup/250 mL basmati rice
2 cups/500 mL water
1/2 Tbsp./7 mL butter or margarine
1 tsp./5 mL salt
2 tsp./10 mL cumin seeds
2-3 Tbsp./10-15 mL canola oil
1 large onion, chopped
1 serrano pepper, chopped
10 cloves
1 tsp./5 mL turmeric powder
1 tsp./5 mL salt
1 cauliflower, cut into florets

In a large pot, combine rice, water, butter and salt and place on high heat. When water starts to boil, reduce heat to low. Cover pot with fitted lid and let simmer for 20 minutes.

In separate frying pan or wok, heat cumin seeds in oil on medium to high heat until they sizzle. Add onion, pepper and cloves. Fry until onions are browned. Add turmeric and salt and cook for another 2-3 minutes.

Add cauliflower to onion and stir-fry for about 10 minutes. If necessary, add additional water to avoid any sticking to bottom of pan. Combine cooked rice and cauliflower. With a large fork, stir until well mixed.

Vikram Vij (left) delights gourmets with his fresh variations on classic Indian dishes.

❦ Direct Delivery: Organics to You and Small Potatoes

It gets easier every day to find organic produce and chemical-free foods—provided you have the time to scour the stores. For those who don't, but who still want to have as healthy a diet as possible, a new generation of grocery delivery services is making it simpler than ever before.

Through his Vancouver company Organics to You, Andrew Capeau brings organic produce right to his customers' doors. Capeau dates his enthusiasm for naturally grown foods from the time he spent working on farms in New Zealand and Australia, where he began to notice that organically raised fare tasted better. Working on conventional farms, he also experienced personally "the amount of chemicals that were sprayed on foods we were about to consume." It took him fifteen minutes every day to scrub the residue from his hands.

Returning to Canada, Capeau borrowed an old van from a friend, acquired some credit and began selling organically raised vegetables door to door. Response was immediate. People were thrilled, he says, at the chance to purchase reasonably priced organic food so easily.

In August 1994, drawing on his existing customer base and the farming contacts he had made, Capeau launched the Grocery Bin. For $33 a week, he delivers a lidded plastic tub brimming with fresh produce—

Surprises land on the doorstep every week for those who subscribe to Andrew Capeau's organic delivery service.

enough to feed one totally vegetarian linebacker or satisfy as many as six average appetites.

"We choose as much B.C.-grown produce as possible," says Capeau, "and we look for varieties that are popular with everyone." Nutritional balance also comes into the picture. Every order includes greens for iron and calcium, fruits for vitamins A and C, and root crops. Every week, a recorded message lists the contents of the current bin. Even in early March, with spring still around the corner, it sounds tempting: "Three pounds of Spartan apples, eight navel oranges, two field tomatoes, one head of green leaf lettuce, one packet of spring salad mix, two pounds of purple-skinned potatoes, two pounds of carrots, one bunch of basil, one pint of cherry tomatoes, one bell pepper, two ruby grapefruit, one bunch of broccoli, one head of celery, and a half-dozen free-range eggs."

In order to maintain a constant clientele, Capeau has made the delivery mechanism as simple as possible. Customers leave a cheque in the mailbox and return home to find the bin on their deck or in the garage. But convenience is only one reason for the popularity of direct delivery services. "The quality really brings people in," Capeau explains. "We're not dealing with food that has sat on shelves or been handled by lots of people. Today it comes from a supplier, tomorrow it's on your doorstep." Building on his success, Capeau is now planning to offer custom boxes assembled from a list of more than three hundred items: "Rice, canned goods, anything that's healthy," he says. Low overhead lets him keep prices competitive.

For Small Potatoes, a Vancouver direct-delivery company launched in 1998, produce is merely the starting point. As well as offering a Fresh Harvest Box of organic fruits and vegetables, the company carries products that are chemical-free and minimally packaged. "We want to support the local economy," says Debra Elliott, who founded Small Potatoes with partner David Van Seters, a consultant in sustainability issues. Jams come from Zebroff Farms in the Okanagan, honey from northern B.C. "Cyoni" orange juice, a product of the Vancouver-based Canadian Youth Orange Network, is squeezed in the morning and delivered later that day.

Small Potatoes' growing number of customers are attracted by the range the company offers. Listed in its catalogue are organic breads, bagels, scones, buns and tortillas. Also available are staples such as cereals, pancake mix, flour, sugar and four different kinds of organic rice. Regular and herbal teas are supplied by the Vancouver Island Tea Factory. Small Potatoes updates the role of the old-time milkman, delivering soy and rice milks, yoghurt, butter, free-range eggs and five kinds of cheese.

Right:

A Vancouver ritual to launch the growing season, Granville Market after Dark links city folk with their farm and fisher counterparts.

Below left:

Wild thimbleberries are free for the foraging.

Below right:

Biodiversity can mean a range of hues, as these organic mushrooms illustrate.

Right and below left:
Roadside shopping beats supermarkets any day. Bedding plants, fresh herbs and salad makings are just some of the treats available at Linnaea Farms on B.C.'s Cortes Island.

Below right:
Wild huckleberries and granola add up to an instant breakfast for campers and other outdoor types.

Customers with a hectic week coming up can ask to have a healthy, fully prepared entrée included in their order. Putting yet another nail in the coffin of the conventional supermarket, Small Potatoes also supplies pet food, household cleaning products and fresh flowers.

Prices, the Small Potatoes catalogue states, are on average lower than those at local grocery stores. Placing a standing order for something brings the item price down by a further 5 per cent. And every second week, the company features a different premium VQA (Vintners Quality Alliance) label wine or beer. All, of course, made in B.C.

More than a dozen home delivery firms have sprung up in Vancouver, Victoria and Toronto over the past decade. Andrew Capeau isn't surprised. "Who the heck *wouldn't* want something that's even fresher delivered to their door at a price comparable to the conventional one?"

ANDREW CAPEAU'S QUICK ZUCCHINI STRING BEANS

6 Tbsp./90 mL olive oil
5 cloves garlic, minced
1 large onion, peeled and sliced
1/4 cup/60 mL tamari or soy sauce, divided into 2 portions
3-4 zucchinis, cut in rounds
2 cups/500 mL string beans, steamed
3 Tbsp./45 mL toasted sesame seeds
1/2 cup/125 mL bread crumbs

Heat oil in a skillet over high heat for 1 minute. Add diced garlic and onion and sauté for 3-4 minutes. Add half the tamari, toss in sliced zucchini and string beans, and stir-fry. Add remaining tamari and cook for 3 minutes. Toss in sesame seeds and bread crumbs, stirring constantly. Cook for an additional 3-4 minutes. Transfer to a serving bowl. *Serves 4-6.*

Storing Fresh Produce

Potatoes should be kept in a cool, dark place, since light exposure will produce a greenish hue on the surface. Called selenium, this is mildly toxic to humans and should not be eaten.

Carrots and beets can be kept for a long time if stored in plastic bags with small holes for ventilation in cold storage or the refrigerator. If you grow vegetables in your own garden, and you don't want to use plastic, keeping your carrots and beets in dirt in cold storage will work very well.

Onions should be stored just below room temperature in a very dry place (except for green onions, which should be refrigerated). Don't put them in plastic bags. Yellow onions have a longer storage life than red ones do.

Salad greens should always be washed before you put them in the fridge. Lightly shake off excess water and place greens in an open plastic bag, leaving plenty of room for them to breathe. Precutting greens and placing them in a sealed plastic container works well too. Use a plastic serrated edge for cutting greens, or tear them by hand; using a metal knife will cause them to turn brown at the edges much faster.

Tomatoes should not be refrigerated; keep them at room temperature in a place that is not too sunny.

Broccoli keeps best in an open plastic bag in the refrigerator.

The East Vancouver Farmers Market

Look at the street plan of any town built a few hundred years ago, and you'll see that it almost always centred on a square. Most days, this was simply an open space. But one day a week—often more—it became the bustling core of the community. Going to market offered people not just a chance to shop and catch up with local news but a constant reminder of the cycle of the seasons.

In Europe, the market tradition is still strong. Most English towns and every French village hold a market at least weekly. By contrast, North American urban design has shunted the buying and selling of food to the outskirts of cities. Today's "market square," coldly lit and silent apart from the muzak filtering in, is the produce section of the supermarket. But buying vegetables from a huge store is a soulless experience, and British Columbia, like many other places across North America, is increasingly taking old-fashioned farmers' markets to its heart.

The Victoria Day weekend marks the first Saturday of the season for the East Vancouver Farmers Market. The air is cold, and people gratefully wrap their hands around hot cups of coffee. Yet even this early in the year, there is produce to be found: a handful of lettuces; pots of sage, thyme and parsley for urban gardens. As the months scroll by, the cornucopia of produce is tipped at an increasingly steeper angle. Out tumble vividly scarlet strawberries. Out roll glossy black cherries so succulent they send up a small fountain of juice when you bite into them. Out come baskets galore of darkly delicious blueberries and rubylike red currants. Lettuces arrive in frilly crimsons and greens, along with crisp green beans, thumb-sized zucchini, lavender sprigs to tuck in with linen and enormous bouquets of sky-blue delphiniums. Peppers, shiny as patent leather, show up not only in the sweet crimson bell varieties but also as wincingly hot habaneros. Stall-holders pass along tips about cooking with unusual vegetables: leek tips and curly garlic tops that look like green hunting horns can both be steamed and eaten like asparagus.

By late summer, the market's stalls are piled high with red, yellow and orange tomatoes, bloomy plums the shade of amber or amethyst, and dark-green and purple kales and cabbages. Pumpkins, onions and squashes striped like fancy hats signal the start of fall, a time to serve up warming stews and casseroles and remember the bounty each new season brings.

How do you start a farmers' market? Plant a seed. Market manager Devorah Kahn was seeking a venue to sell her home-grown tomato seedlings when she attended a forum on farmers' markets in early 1995. All in attendance came away inspired, and nine people—all from the same East Vancouver neighbourhood—got busy. "We spent five months working our tails off," Kahn remembers. Finding a suitable site, lobbying city council, meeting the requirements of the city's health department: getting the market up and running was a lengthy and arduous process. Licensed initially on a trial basis, it now operates in a parking lot at Vancouver's Trout Lake on a year-to-year basis.

A community economic development grant from VanCity Credit Union and stall fees provided first-year funding for the market; these days stall fees, fund-raisers and a number of small grants pay Kahn's salary and cover costs such as advertising and liability insurance.

Kahn always knew that attracting customers would be easy, but at first "farmers weren't convinced it would be worth their while. We had no history, and it meant a day off the farm." But it didn't

Organizing a Farmers' Market

If you don't have a farmers' market in your area, you might want to organize one. Here are some tips to get you started:

- If you can, visit a few other farmers' markets to see how they are set up. Talk to organizers and stall-holders. Ask what works for them and what they would change if they were starting again.
- Hold a public meeting to gauge interest in your community. You might want to invite a speaker from another market to answer people's questions.
- Form a committee to spearhead action. Contact your local municipality about what is required to get a permit. Hurdles are many, so be prepared. Getting someone from the health department on your committee will help move the process along.
- Decide who will be participating. At the East Vancouver Farmers Market, 60 per cent of the stalls are agricultural, 20 per cent sell crafts and 20 per cent sell prepared food, with the stipulation that everything must be grown or made by the stall-holders themselves. Although each market is different, you can save time by borrowing guidelines from other markets and adapting them to your situation.
- Investigate funding possibilities. Grants from credit unions, local churches and other interested groups can provide the necessary money for start-up expenses and ensure community support.
- Use handbills, posters and public service announcements to get the word out.
- Farmers' markets are as much about building community as they are about providing access to healthy, nutritious and locally grown food. Encourage people to think about the market as a place to publicize upcoming events, give out information or showcase local performers.

take long for growers to change their minds. A thousand people attended the market's first day in July 1995, and the produce sold out in two hours. "One farmer called his wife to pick up more produce and bring it in. You don't get much fresher than that," Kahn says. By the following Saturday, the number of farmers had doubled.

Stall-holders also sell the hand-crafted pots, mobiles, platters and jewellery they make over the winter—and the baked goods they've made that very morning. For some it's a hobby or a chance to make an extra bit of money; for others, it's a full-time profession. Under the banner "Mum's Muffins" (she collaborates with her mother, Francesca Newton-Moss), Janie Newton-Moss sets out muffins, scones, dried-fruit breads and more, all made using organic "and certainly unprocessed" ingredients as much as possible. A former social worker, Newton-Moss now teaches cooking classes and does catering, a career switch she says was made possible largely by her experiences at the market. "There are only so many times friends and relations can test recipes," says Newton-Moss. "It was a very positive transition." But markets do more than change individual lives, she maintains. "I mourn the loss of neighbourhoods. The market is a focal point of our community that connects us with our rural roots."

Those who nibble their way around the market eventually meet Deborah Lawrence, too. Ten months of the year, she is a preschool teacher. During the summer, she is behind a stall filled with pies, scones, cookies, brownies, pickles, preserves and relishes, all home-made. "I've always wanted to do this," says Lawrence, "but running a store costs money." The camaraderie of the market is as important to her as the additional income. Her least favourite part of running her own business? "Baking at four in the morning."

Don Schultz has a year-round full-time job, but every summer Saturday finds him at the market manning his Big Don's Homemade Pickles stall. Since the early eighties, Schultz has simmered his recipes down to a half-dozen proven favourites, among them superb pickled beets and addictive green tomato chow-chow. He aims to fill three hundred dozen jars each season and donates all his net profits to charity.

The market is a scene filled with happy dogs, fiddle players and face-painting. A stall-holder explains the difference between wild-flower and clover honey as he offers samples. Shoppers originally from Italy and Britain compare the way each nation cooks potatoes. Amateur chefs surround one stand, eager to pick up the free recipe for strawberry vinegar, and at the back-yard garden table is a woman whose zucchini crop was just too successful this year.

Buying, selling and exchanging information are only part of what a market is all about. There are few other places where consumers have the chance to rediscover the pure deliciousness of fresh food at its peak. Above all, it's a reaffirmation of community. No one talks to strangers in a supermarket. At a farmers' market, everyone does.

MARA JERNIGAN'S LINGUINE WITH ZUCCHINI RIBBONS, LEMON THYME AND PARMESAN

1 large zucchini
2 oz./60 g unsalted butter
1 tsp./5 mL garlic, minced
4 Tbsp./60 mL fresh lemon thyme, stemmed and finely chopped
1 lb./500 g dried Italian linguine
1/4 cup/60 mL Italian parmesan cheese, freshly grated
salt and freshly ground pepper to taste

Slice zucchini into thin slices lengthwise and trim into 1/2"/1 cm ribbons, 6-8" long.

Heat a large frying pan over medium-high heat. Add butter and garlic and sauté until translucent. Add zucchini ribbons, seasoning with a pinch of salt. Sauté until soft but not mushy. Add lemon thyme, toss in pan and remove from heat.

Bring a large pot of salted water to the boil. Cook linguine according to package directions, about 7 minutes. Drain well and add to zucchini mixture.

Return to heat and sprinkle pan evenly with parmesan. Toss well to coat and warm through. Season with salt and pepper and serve immediately. *Serves 4.*

KRISHNA JAMAL'S **INDIAN ROAST POTATOES**

Executive chef at Rubina Tandoori, one of Canada's foremost Indian restaurants, Krishna Jamal learned traditional techniques while growing up in what is now Tanzania. As a restaurateur in London, England, and later Vancouver, she has committed herself to perfecting Indian dishes from the subcontinent and beyond. As a teacher and writer, she takes keen amateur chefs on engrossing—and spicy—explorations of her native cuisine.

2 tsp./10 mL coriander seeds
1 Tbsp./15 mL cumin seeds
2 tsp./10 mL red chili flakes, or to taste
1 Tbsp./15 mL vegetable oil
1 tsp./5 mL mustard seeds, preferably black
2-3 cloves garlic, crushed
1 tsp./5 mL ground turmeric
1/2 tsp./2 mL salt
1 1/2 lb./750 g nugget new potatoes

Preheat oven to 350°F/180°C.

Toast coriander seeds, cumin seeds and chili flakes in unoiled pan over low heat until fragrant. Crush with rolling pin.

Heat a large pan over high heat. Add oil and mustard seeds. When seeds start to pop, reduce heat to medium and add crushed spice mixture, garlic, turmeric and salt. Cook for 3 minutes. Add potatoes and toss well. Make sure potatoes are evenly coated.

Place in unoiled baking pan, cover with foil and bake for 25 minutes, or until potatoes are tender. Test for doneness with knife. Eat immediately. *Serves 4-5.*

✿ Friesen Farm

Farming isn't a nine-to-five job that lets you take off every weekend. In the growing months, a farm keeps you running almost constantly. So where do you find the time to bring your goods to market? You can either stay home and hoe your vegetables, or load up your truck and head into town—but you can't do both.

That's why Fraser Valley farmer Ann Friesen works with others to market her produce. She belongs to three groups, each an alliance of farmers who have banded together in order to sell what they grow. Better Choice Organics supplies wholesalers, home delivery companies and stores; Langley Organic Growers sends produce to market in Mission and East Vancouver; and Valley Organic Farmers shows up at Vancouver's Granville Island Public Market.

Ann Friesen grew up on a 150-acre spread in Ontario, where her parents raised horses, cattle and chickens. Today she and her husband, Albert, run his family farm. The two didn't set out to be farmers, but what began as a hobby evolved into a five-acre organic market garden. Soon the couple took on pure-bred Herefords as well, raising heifers for breeding stock and steers for meat and leasing thirty-five more acres to grow cattle feed. They started to plant organic lettuce, arugula, kale and mustard greens, some of which they supplied to the Glorious Garnish and Seasonal Salad Company, where Albert had worked for a year. Before long they teamed up with other growers under the banner of Valley Organic Farmers in order to offer consumers a far wider variety of vegetables than any individual farmer could supply.

Linking in with a B.C. Ministry of Agriculture project colloquially known as DATE (officially Demonstration of Agricultural Technology and Economics) was the first stage in a new co-operative venture. The project's goal was to establish markets throughout B.C. for products grown locally using environmentally friendly practices. The ministry provided fertilizer and plants; the farmers provided the labour.

Things got underway in 1995. The Fraser Valley group's initial plan was to bring celery, a

Ann Friesen gets together with other local farmers to bring produce to the city.

crop that's difficult to grow organically, to market over the summer, explains Ann Friesen. Four farms grew celery, planting it in rotation every two weeks; there were three plantings in all, timed so that the market supply was continuous. Friesen Farm purchased the equipment needed to wash and trim the celery, and everyone else came there to use it. "And one farmer owned the truck we used to ship it out," says Ann. The group learned as they went—"The first large shipment, we didn't know how to invoice," Ann remembers. They didn't have a name, either, so people stood around the truck and brain-stormed. That's how Better Choice Organics was born.

The joint experiment worked so well that the group decided to continue co-operatively. "It lets you centralize sales," says Friesen, "and we only need one truck. The farmers can farm instead of sitting on the phone and driving around Vancouver." Working together also allows the group to offer consistency and volume to customers throughout the growing season, an important factor in regaining the market share from imports. Albert's mother, Ivy Friesen, is pleased to see people returning to the food she grew up on. "We lived out of our garden in the summer," she recalls. "We had goats for milk, and chickens for meat. We lived healthier then."

These days, Better Choice Organics comprises five participants, each of whom specializes in a particular product. One farmer grows broccoli and cauliflower; another harvests celery, berries and artichokes. The Friesens concentrate on salad greens. Their neighbours raise lettuce, radishes, spinach and some beets, and a farmer who owns a greenhouse contributes cucumbers and tomatoes.

Better Choice is run from Friesen Farm, which is also the central drop-off point for produce. Participants have collectively funded a cooler. Three times a week, the Better Choice Organics truck heads into the city on its delivery rounds. Everyone else in the group stays home—and gets on with their work at the farm.

ANN FRIESEN'S **ARUGULA PESTO**

2 cloves garlic
2 cups/500 mL arugula, packed
1/2 cup/125 mL pine nuts
1/3 cup/80 mL parmesan cheese
1/2 cup/125 mL olive oil
salt and pepper to taste

Chop garlic in a food processor. Add arugula, pine nuts and parmesan cheese and process until well blended. Add olive oil in a slow stream until a wet paste is obtained. Season with salt and pepper. *Makes about 3 cups/750 mL.*

FRANK PABST'S **ASPARAGUS AND ARUGULA SALAD WITH SHALLOT AND TARRAGON VINAIGRETTE**

Frank Pabst is chef de cuisine at Vancouver's Lumière, where he and chef Robert Feenie employ a combination of sparklingly fresh ingredients and authentic French cooking techniques that has led to multiple awards and international recognition.

8 stalks asparagus (white if available)
pinch salt
1 Tbsp./15 mL sugar
7 Tbsp./105 g fresh morels or other
    wild mushrooms
1 Tbsp. /15 mL olive oil
salt and pepper to taste
1 shallot, minced
1 Tbsp./15 mL fresh tarragon, minced
1 tsp./5 mL Dijon mustard
1 Tbsp./15 mL lemon juice
3 Tbsp./45 mL sherry vinegar
6 Tbsp./90 mL extra virgin olive oil
sea salt and freshly ground pepper
4 Tbsp./60 g fresh fava beans, blanched and peeled
2 cups/500 mL arugula (take off large stems)
5 Tbsp./75 g prosciutto, very thinly sliced
    (duck if available)
1 1/2 Tbsp./22 g parmesan shavings

Peel asparagus, starting just underneath the tip. Add salt and sugar to water, bring to a boil and blanch asparagus for 6 minutes. Cut each asparagus stalk in 3 pieces.

Cut mushrooms in half and rinse in cold water. Lightly sauté in olive oil, salt and pepper. Remove mushrooms.

Combine mushroom juice with shallots, tarragon, mustard, lemon juice and sherry vinegar. Whisk in olive oil and adjust seasoning with salt and pepper.

Combine asparagus, fava beans, mushrooms and arugula in a salad bowl, add vinaigrette and mix carefully. Garnish each plate with prosciutto and parmesan shavings. *Serves 4.*

VI. Celebrating

Before the Hallmark greeting card era; **before** every possible celebration was made into a commercial opportunity; before retailers maxed out on the existing holidays and new ones had to be invented—before all of that, people around the world honoured the times that were important in their lives.

We feast because the seasons change, and because there are things beyond our ken that we wish to respect and acknowledge. We raise a toast when someone new comes into our lives or to say good-bye to someone who is no longer with us. By sharing food on these occasions we learn about different cultures and traditions and find in them our common humanity.

Most of us now reside in suburban and urban rather than rural settings, but it is impossible to fully appreciate either landscape without having experienced the other. Some celebrations bring the cornucopia of what the country has to offer to the population centres. Others, held right on food-producing lands, remind us of our roots. Country celebrations are not purely nostalgic, however; rural areas still provide us with food, fresh air, water, green space and a value system different from that in the major cities.

Celebrations feed our bodies and our spirits. They give us a chance to express both appreciation for what we have today and the hope that things in the future will be as good or even better. This final chapter of *Farm Folk, City Folk* features city and country celebrations; in both places people gather to celebrate the passing of the seasons and the passages of their lives. We also include a

menu of recipes showcasing regional ingredients that add up to a spectacular feast.

To your health, *salud, l'chayim, skål, prosit...*

—H.B.

❦ City Celebrations

Every year, from late spring until early fall, cities and towns across British Columbia come vibrantly alive with outdoor events that celebrate the province's bounty. Corn bought from roadside stands stars at neighbourhood barbecues. Salmon dinners held in city-centre parks raise money for local theatre companies, and regional festivals shine the spotlight on that year's crop of strawberries or blackberries.

With its large population of people drawn from all over the planet, Vancouver is no exception. Height-of-summer jam and pickle contests at the East Vancouver Farmers Market attract entrants by the score. The Vancouver Folk Music Festival, held each July at Jericho Beach, draws almost as many attendees for the food—Hornby Island Pizza, spicy Ethiopian fare from the Nyala African Hotspot, delicious deep-fried "whales' tails"—as for the music. Every B.C. Day long weekend, Oppenheimer Park fills to capacity for the annual Powell Street Festival, hosted by

Above and bottom:
Kicking off the growing season at Granville Island's Market after Dark.

Vancouver's Japanese residents; it's a colourful mix of cultural events, martial arts, craft displays and delicious foods such as takoyaki (grilled dough balls wrapped around chunks of octopus), yaki onigiri (barbecued rice balls) and teriyaki salmon. Late in the summer, the Botanical Garden at the University of British Columbia hosts an annual apple festival, with dozens of different varieties on display.

Stone Soup, held annually at the Britannia Community Services Centre in East Vancouver, is both an upbeat springtime celebration of freshness and taste and a chance for those who

attend to explore the issues connected with food. Music from a live band sets the mood. Master gardeners provide information on what kinds of cabbages will flourish in Vancouver soil and how to keep insects away without harming the environment. Food vendors offer fresh-baked muffins and breads; farmers bring along their first crop of tomatoes, peppers and asparagus. Inside the community centre are free workshops on biotechnology and easy-to-grow kitchen crops, as well as demonstrations of beekeeping and worm-composting. For people whose "land" may be a window box or a flower pot or two, it's an opportunity to learn more about the glorious food their region produces.

Market after Dark, held at the Granville Island Public Market, is another city celebration that narrows the gap between what we eat and those who produce it. A fund-raiser for the food advocacy organization FarmFolk/CityFolk, it is held on a Monday evening in May in the vast, banner-hung market building, which comes alive with stall-holders and shoppers seven days of the week in summer, every day but Monday the rest of the time.

The line-ups start early for Market after Dark, and by six o'clock the aisles are swarming with hungry people. A chef deftly sears chunks of B.C. salmon in a sizzling hot pan, squeezes an orange over the fish and serves it to those who have now learned the "recipe" and are keen to discover how it tastes. Children clamour for chocolate-dipped strawberries and sharpen emerging gourmet tastebuds on pizza topped with sun-dried tomatoes and artichokes or spinach, garlic and feta

cheese. A local purveyor of exotic beverages sells a tangy infusion of Saskatoon berries. One of the market's permanent tenants, a bakery, offers wedges of green olive bread, apple and cheese focaccia, and half a dozen other varieties. Several local brewing companies have tasters on hand of their ales and lagers, some of which are named after local sites or neighbourhoods. A vineyard has brought along its Chardonnay, Merlot and Pinots.

There are people to talk to, displays to browse and pamphlets to take home. The curious can find out why concern for how our food is produced is steadily increasing, or exactly what makes a vegetable organic, or what a sustainable food system might look like. And these few hours of grazing have brought home to them in the most vivid possible way why all this is important. Buying and eating local food picked in its prime means not only great flavour but a healthy, thriving community.

Mebrat and Assefa Kebede's authentic Ethiopian cooking blends ancient techniques with locally grown ingredients at Market after Dark.

❦ A Celebration Menu

LISA ROWSON'S **ROASTED TOMATO SOUP WITH CILANTRO PESTO**

Lisa Rowson is a former chef at the Tomato Fresh Food Café, Diane Clement's dynamic and funky Vancouver eatery. A former Olympic sprinter and winner of a bronze medal at the 1958 Commonwealth Games, Clement has long been an advocate of fresh cuisine that relies on great ingredients for its impact.

SOUP

2 lbs./1 kg fresh tomatoes (roma or other paste variety)
8 cloves garlic, minced
sea salt and pepper
2 Tbsp./30 mL extra virgin olive oil
1 medium onion
2 tsp./10 mL ground cumin (preferably fresh-ground from toasted whole cumin seeds)
2 Tbsp./30 mL red wine vinegar

Preheat oven to 350°F/180°C.

Remove core and quarter tomatoes. Lay cut side up on a baking sheet along with garlic cloves. Sprinkle with sea salt and pepper and drizzle with olive oil. Bake for 10 minutes. Reduce heat and continue cooking until tomatoes have released most of their pulp and are nicely roasted.

In a pot over low heat, sauté onion and cumin. Cook for 15-20 minutes or until onion is soft and slightly caramelized. Add roasted tomatoes and garlic. Pour in vinegar and simmer for 10 minutes. Transfer to a food processor and pulse until a smooth soup is obtained. Season with salt and pepper.

PESTO

1 bunch cilantro
1 Tbsp./15 mL parsley, chopped
1 clove garlic, minced
2-4 Tbsp./30-60 mL extra virgin olive oil

Combine all ingredients in a food processor. Season with salt and pepper and reserve for garnish.

TOMATO BOWL

Hollow out 4 beefsteak tomatoes and chill. Fill with soup and top with a dollop of pesto. Garnish with toasted tortilla chips. Can be served hot or cold. *Serves 4.*

KAI LERMAN'S **MESCLUN GREENS WITH FRESH HERBS, AVOCADO, SMOKED CHICKEN AND RASPBERRY DRESSING**

German-born Kai Lerman began his career at the age of sixteen, apprenticing under some of Europe's top names, including French master chef Marc Haeberlin. "Wherever I've worked, I've used the ingredients produced in the region," says Lerman, now executive chef at Vancouver's Sutton Place Hotel. "It's so much better to use what is available locally than importing it. Fish, beautiful game, fruit: we have so much here in B.C."

VINAIGRETTE

4 Tbsp./60 mL raspberry vinegar
1 Tbsp./15 mL honey
2 Tbsp./30 mL chicken stock
salt and pepper
1/2 cup/125 mL fresh raspberries
1 Tbsp./15 mL dry vermouth
1/2 cup/125 mL sunflower oil

Combine all ingredients, with the exception of oil, in a blender and mix until berries are puréed. Slowly add oil and season to taste. Set aside.

GREENS

4 cups/1 L mesclun greens
small handful fresh herbs: tarragon, lemon balm, Italian parsley (strip leaves off stems)
2 avocados, sliced
2 smoked chicken breasts, shredded

Fan out avocado pieces on individual plates. In a bowl, toss greens with some of the vinaigrette. Add fresh herbs and shredded chicken. Loosely mix together and place decoratively around avocado pieces. Drizzle with raspberry vinaigrette to taste. *Serves 4.*

MARA JERNIGAN'S **PAN-SEARED MUSCOVY DUCK BREAST**

2 large Muscovy duck breasts
$^1/_2$ cup/125 mL rich duck or veal stock (plus approx. 2 Tbsp./30 mL for later)
$^1/_4$ cup/60 mL fireweed honey
3 Tbsp./45 mL Venturi-Schulze balsamico or other top-quality balsamic vinegar
2 Tbsp./30 mL olive oil
$^1/_2$ tsp./2 mL fresh thyme or rosemary, finely chopped
salt and freshly ground pepper to taste

Preheat oven to 425°F/220°C.

Remove white tendons and sinew from the flesh side of each duck breast. Flip over and, with a sharp knife, score halfway through skin and fat of each breast. Repeat from opposite direction to make a criss-cross pattern on skin.

Heat a small saucepan over medium-high heat, add honey, and heat until honey turns a rich brown. Deglaze pan quickly with half of vinegar.

Reduce heat to medium and add stock. Dissolve caramel and cook until reduced by half. (Sauce should easily coat the back of a spoon.) Keep warm and set aside.

Heat an oven-proof skillet over high heat for 1 minute. Add olive oil and heat until oil is very hot. Add duck skin-side down and sear fat from breasts. Reduce heat and cook breasts for 3-4 minutes, or until skin is golden brown. Flip breasts over and quickly sear the flesh side.

Flip breasts back to skin side and transfer skillet to the oven. Roast for 6-8 minutes for medium-rare. Breasts will bounce back lightly to the touch but remain juicy. Transfer to a plate and rest for 6-8 minutes in a warm spot.

Return skillet to stovetop. (Don't forget, the handle is hot!) Drain off excess fat and deglaze with remaining vinegar and 2 Tbsp./30 mL of stock. Scrape bottom of pan with a wooden spoon to release pan drippings. Add mixture to reserved sauce, strain through a fine strainer and skim any excess fat from the surface. Add minced herb to sauce and season to taste.

Slice duck breasts across the width on an angle. Serve with potatoes roasted in duck fat, seasonal vegetables and sauce. *Serves 4.*

BILL JONES'S **PINE MUSHROOMS AND SWEET CORN POLENTA**

Pine mushrooms are very pungent, so one or two small mushrooms are all you need to infuse the polenta with rich flavour. If you are using other kinds of mushrooms, I would suggest adding up to 1 lb./500 g.

6 cups/1.5 L water or stock
1 Tbsp./15 mL salt
2 cups/500 mL cornmeal, stone-ground
2 cups/500 mL fresh or frozen corn kernels
2-3 oz./60-85 g pine mushrooms *(Tricholoma ponderosum)*, thinly sliced
2 Tbsp./30 mL minced fresh herbs (rosemary, marjoram, parsley, lovage, sage, thyme, etc.)
2 Tbsp./30 mL butter
2 Tbsp./30 mL extra virgin olive oil
1/2 cup/125 mL parmesan cheese, grated
salt and pepper

In a thick-bottomed pot, heat water and salt to a boil. Add cornmeal in a slow stream while constantly stirring. Reduce heat and stir until mixture thickens into a solid mass and cornmeal grains have softened (about 15 minutes). Gradually add water or stock, stirring constantly to thin cornmeal into a soft paste.

Add corn kernels and pine mushrooms, and cook for an additional 3-4 minutes. Thin with stock or water to make a soft mass.

Remove pot from stove and add herbs, butter, olive oil and parmesan cheese. Season well with salt and pepper. *Serves 4-6.*

GREG HOOK'S **FROZEN WHITE CHOCOLATE TERRINE WITH DRIED CRANBERRIES AND BASIL**

1/2 cup/125 mL dried cranberries
2 Tbsp./30 mL Grand Marnier
1 Tbsp./15 mL water
1 Tbsp./15 mL sugar
1 cup/250 mL whipping cream
6 egg yolks
1/3 cup/80 mL basil leaves (packed), chopped fine
1/4 vanilla bean
1 cup/250 mL light cream
3/4 lb./375 g white chocolate, chopped fine
juice of 1 lemon
chocolate sauce for garnish (see recipe p. 109)
whipped cream for garnish
chopped pistachios for garnish

Put cranberries, Grand Marnier, water and sugar into a pan and heat until liquid is absorbed. Set aside.

Prepare an 8"/20 cm loaf tin by brushing it with a thin layer of vegetable oil. Press in plastic film, making sure that no ridges remain and tin is completely lined.

Whip cream to soft peaks and set in fridge. Whisk egg yolks until pale yellow and well mixed.

Split vanilla bean and scrape seeds into light cream. Add basil and bring light cream to a boil. When light cream mixture starts to boil, pour one-third of it onto the yolks, stir, and then pour yolk mixture slowly back into light cream mixture. Take pot off heat and stir continually until mixture thickens slightly. Do not boil, or mixture will curdle. (This is made in same manner as crème Anglaise; however, as it has no sugar, it will curdle more easily).

Place chocolate in a bowl and pour light cream mixture on top. Stir until chocolate is melted. Add lemon juice and cranberry mixture. Stir well. Fold in whipped cream and pour into the lined mould. Wrap with a piece of plastic wrap.

Set in freezer for at least 3-4 hours. When frozen, remove terrine from freezer and then remove from the tin. (You may need to dip tin into a sink of warm water for a moment to loosen sides). Wrap well. Keep in freezer until needed. Terrine may be kept up to a week if well-wrapped.

To serve, unwrap terrine and cut into thick slices. Cut each piece diagonally to form 2 triangular pieces. Lay one piece on a plate and stand the second on its side. Pour warm chocolate sauce at side of terrine and add lightly whipped cream if desired as garnish. Sprinkle crushed pistachios on the chocolate sauce. *Serves 4-6.*

❦ Country Celebrations

Living close to the earth as they do, country-dwellers are always aware of the magic of the growing cycle: the tiny seeds that beget small spears of green; the ripening fruit that guarantees food for the chilly months ahead and provides new seed for the following spring. No wonder that the planting and harvesting of the food we eat have been celebrated for centuries all around the world.

Fraser Common Farm in B.C.'s Fraser Valley has developed its own rites of merrymaking over the years. The farm's spring equinox celebration, held at sunrise, is very much a family affair. It's a chance for those who live and work at the farm, and their friends and relatives, to come together for feasting and fun. People stay overnight at the farm, then set to work before dawn making Easter bonnets from

newsprint, streamers and sparkly trims. Suitably clad, celebrants parade along the farm's main pathway, singing as they go and offering a specially encouraging ditty to the chickens en route. Afterwards, back at the farmhouse, all sit down for a huge breakfast of pancakes made with eggs gathered that morning. The first crop of rhubarb gives its clean tartness to a sauce. For those who prefer savoury side dishes, there is a soup made with young green nettles. Spring has been officially welcomed.

The fall equinox event, Fraser Common's version of harvest festival, is a day of busyness, of putting up and putting by for the barren months to come. Apples are sliced for drying, made into applesauce or pressed to make juice. As people work, a fire is lit, and huge cauldrons of water are put on to boil. In late afternoon a shout goes up. Loaded with fresh-picked corn, sweet and milky, the van is back from nearby Friesen Farm. Some of the cobs are boiled, some are soaked in water and then baked in the coals. Dishes and platters are set out for a potluck supper, and everyone sits down to eat, heaping their plates with just-picked salad and slices of cake sweet with fruit and chunky with hazelnuts.

Another annual Fraser Common event gets its inspiration from Japan. Each August, Michael Marrapese hosts a moon-viewing party for thirty or forty friends at the farm. He prepares dishes that feature the five methods of food preparation basic to Japanese cuisine—deep-frying, steaming, simmering, grilling and preserving. A glowing barbecue holds kebabs of chicken, tofu and vegetables. A giant bowl brims with chilled slippery noodles for the salad known as sunomono. Smaller bowls hold grilled shiitake mushrooms, green beans in a brown sauce, seaweed from a local Japanese grocery store, black sesame seeds and pickled daikon. There are also—a decidedly western touch—yellow, orange and red nasturtium blossoms and purple chive flowers. On the two-burner Coleman stove sits a big pot of soup to be poured on the miso and garnished at will. In a steamer are tiny plump squash, yellow and green, stuffed with chopped mushrooms, ginger and garlic.

Some years the sky is clear and the moon rises fat and full like a huge serene pearl. Other years, it stays shyly behind the clouds. As the day dims, kerosene lamps are lit. Marrapese puts the finishing touches on the meal, mixing rice to make vegetable maki rolls. Dessert is flower-shaped cutouts of mulberry jelly made with farm-grown berries.

The feasting over, guests sit around on bales of hay, shrugging their collars up around their ears to fend off the night breezes. Someone brings out a guitar. Traditionally, the musical program is simple: any song with the word "moon" in it. It is dark as pitch as guests leave the pasture and make their way back through the woods guided by two rows of tea lights gleaming like miniature moons.

A month or so later, guests are back at the farm for the biggest celebration on Fraser Common Farm's calendar. Every year since 1995, on a mid-September Sunday, the farm plays host to Feast of Fields, at which growers, chefs, winemakers and the general public gather to mingle, taste and sip the best of what's local, raising funds for FarmFolk/CityFolk in the process.

The city folk are relaxed after their drive along the winding roads of the valley. As they arrive, each person is handed a wineglass, a napkin (which can double as a bib) and a map showing them who is cooking what. The farm is dressed up for the day. Tent poles wrapped

in vines and decorated with orange rowan berries look like a detail from a mediaeval tapestry. Crisp as a new apple, the fall air is cool enough to make the first dish—a spicy salmon Indian-fusion soup—a welcome one. A local bakery offers fig and anise bread and chewy slabs of rosemary foccacia. One table features rows of scallop shells filled with a salad of nasturtium leaves, fennel, arugula and tarragon. Individual farmers have teamed up with specific restaurants to show off their best.

As people wander back and forth, word spreads quickly: of miniature pita breads crammed with greens, some peppery, some lemony, every bite different; of fiery vegetable curry; of the unutterably wicked dessert—part hazelnuts, part toffee, part cream—to be earmarked as a grand finale to all the nibbling.

The food is as sophisticated as anything they can find in the city, but attendees are clearly enjoying the surrounding countryside. Glimpsed between the tents are pastoral vignettes of barns and fields and Holstein cows. Lively fiddle music plays among the trees, calling the crowd to the upper pasture. Sun filters through the leaves as people saunter along the path past the rows of purple kale, arugula and pole beans.

Swags of chrome-yellow marigolds and feathery dill drape the edges of the white-clothed tables. At one, a grower explains his varietal tomatoes—including Yellow Stuffers, which look like yellow peppers—and pares off chunks for people to try. At another stall, purple and green grapes are piled high on a three-tiered stand, with bunches laid out on the table for sampling. So is a bowl of what one taster calls "Cape gooseberries" and another "ground cherries." Most people do not even know what to expect as they peel the brown, papery covering off the small yellow fruit (a relative of the more familiar tomatillo) and experience its sweet, custardlike flavour for the first time.

In the chicken run, hens peck avidly at tiny pumpkin shells that

earlier held soup or grab at pieces of bread proffered by curious children. Beside one table, oyster shells pile up as in a midden. Much of the cuisine is West Coast contemporary in style, but not all. Leaping back in time are several hearty preparations of grains and legumes that incorporate local cabbage and carrots.

Guests sip, savour and compare notes as wineries pour the new vintage of Pinot Blanc or Chardonnay. Hosts wearing white chefs' coats tour visitors through the farm's gardens. Local authors autograph cookbooks and discuss the more finicky details of recipes with avid amateurs. Eventually the sun slides down behind the hill.

Replete and relaxed, the city folk go home, knowing far more than they did when they arrived about what the farm folk do.

The FarmFolk/CityFolk Society:
Celebrating, Educating, Advocating, Taking Action

FarmFolk/CityFolk is a food advocacy organization. The force that drives us is a desire to change the world in which we live: to learn and teach others how to care for the earth, conserve its resources and create a socially just society. Today, grocery stores and restaurants across North America are full of beautiful, fresh, healthy and nutritious things to eat. We want to ensure that future generations have the same wonderful access we enjoy.

Not so long ago more than 50 per cent of the North American population lived on farms. Now, only three generations later, just over 1 per cent of us are farmers. This estrangement of people from the land creates health, social and environmental problems. At FarmFolk/CityFolk, we work to bring people closer to the sources of their food. We initiate and support actions aimed at creating a food system that produces and distributes healthy, nutritious, safe, affordable food in sufficient quantities that no one need go hungry. We also want the production and distribution of this food to provide meaningful work with reasonable pay and good working conditions.

FarmFolk/CityFolk would like to see agriculture actively following a sustainable, ecologically sound and health-producing model; we believe that permaculture is the best way to achieve this. We unite poverty issues with land use planning and development so that both include food production. We connect food with celebration. In our view, health, social justice, and environmental and economic sustainability are mutually dependent.

FarmFolk/CityFolk's members and supporters represent a broad spectrum of the community, including farmers, growers, market gardeners, health professionals, politicians, bureaucrats, corporate leaders, academics, wholesalers, retailers, restaurateurs, marketers, marketing boards, community organizations, international development organizations and organic producer associations. We serve as a catalyst, a resource agency and a clearinghouse. Most importantly, FarmFolk/CityFolk starts conversations. We put food on the agenda of health groups and social justice on the agenda of farm groups; we bring environment together with agriculture to further the goal of creating a just society. We uncover and articulate the questions we think are most critical to ask.

FarmFolk/CityFolk works on a wellness model, looking at the underlying problem rather than attacking symptoms. Healthy food is central to humanity: without it, we cannot survive. And without sustainable societies, the earth that nourishes us will not survive either. Our work proceeds on the local level to affect the global, and we apply lessons learned at the global level to our communities.

Most people in the more affluent nations eat on average three times a day, every day, or more than a thousand times a year. Each of these meals presents an opportunity to remind eaters of basic principles and facts about all aspects of the food chain. FarmFolk/CityFolk subscribes to Ralph Nader's assertion that it only takes an informed and mobilized 1 per cent of the population to achieve monumental social change. We believe far more people than that see the need for change and understand, on a fundamental level, what kind of change is needed. Linking, co-ordinating, mobilizing and analyzing: this is what we are all about.

For more information, contact us at:

FarmFolk / CityFolk Society
208 - 2211 West 4th Avenue
Vancouver, British Columbia V6K 4S2
604-730-0450 (phone)
604-730-0451 (fax)
Toll free in B.C. 1-888-730-0452
e-mail: office@ffcf.bc.ca

Visit our website at http://www.ffcf.bc.ca

FarmFolk/CityFolk Society
106-131 Water Street
Vancouver, BC
V6B 4M3 Canada

Index